MOTIVATION WITHOUT THE ~~hype~~.

UNLEASH YOUR GREATNESS AND BUILD AN A-Z APPROACH TO LIVING AN EPIC LIFE

GEZ PEREZ

Copyright © 2019 Gez Perez

All rights reserved. No part of this publication may be reproduced, distributed, or transmitted in any form or by any means, including photocopying, recording, or other electronic or mechanical methods, without the prior written permission of the publisher, except in the case of brief quotations embodied in reviews and certain other non-commercial uses permitted by copyright law.

Paperback ISBN: 978-1-925638-47-9
Digital ISBN: 978-1-925638-48-6

DEDICATION

This book is for my amazing family who has been an incredible support throughout my journey in writing this book and building my career and business. To my kids Judah and Jireh who are the reason of motivation, and my beautiful wife Hannah from whom I have learned so much about the importance of love and family—you're my absolute inspiration and greatest supporters.

This book is also for my close friends and associates who have encouraged me and continued to display their passion, patience and purpose. Plus never stopped believing in me.

CONTENTS

Dedication 2
Motivation without the Hype 7

PART 1: GREATNESS STARTS WITH SELF-AWARNESS 13
1 It's a New Day 15
2 Battle of the Minds 27
3 Getting into your Lane 41
4 Live Life on Principles 55

PART 2: GREATNESS IS ALL ABOUT EXCELLENCE 67
5 Bring in the Standards 69
6 Develop a Hybrid System 79
7 Protect the Culture Vibe 97
8 Eye of the Tiger 109

PART 3: GREATNESS IS GRATITUDE & PERSPECTIVE 123
9 Rise in your Inner 125
10 Conquer in your Outer 137
11 Be the Bigger Person 151
12 Follow through in Action 159

13 **BONUS: 21 Days of Thrive Challenge** 169
   About Gez Perez 193
   Programs by Gez Perez 195
   Thrive Forward Coaching Program 196

INTRODUCTION

MOTIVATION WITHOUT THE HYPE!

It was in 2013 that a huge light bulb happened in my life—or maybe I should say a lightning bolt hit me that If I was to be successful in life, I can't make excuses but only take action.

Living in the mundaneness of life is not cool. You get stuck in all forms and shapes when it comes to life. You push two steps forward and suddenly you fall five steps backwards. It sounds dramatic, I know, but in most cases it happens. When speaking about setbacks, there was a point in time when I felt the struggle was real. When your own problems and challenges are combined with family situations which don't sit well. I normally don't talk much on family matters and I realize at the end of the tunnel there is always victory when you choose your outcomes.

NOTHING MATTERS EXCEPT FOR MOM

In 2005, my mom was diagnosed with stage three breast cancer. I still remember the feeling that nothing mattered in the world but my mom.

Your mind goes into overdrive and questions gets filtered into your mind. Should you remain optimistic, positive, or should you freak out and panic?

I know for a fact my dad was concerned about my mom and understandably because he is the husband of my mother, even though he religiously believed in God and had faith that everything would be ok.

My mom was a fighter, warrior, and an absolute ninja. She held her composure with such optimism and positivity that her faith inspired her to live. As a result she conquered breast cancer twice.

If there's one lesson I can draw to this, is the mentality she brought into her life and these three affirmation words: "I CAN! I WILL! I MUST!"

I'm a family of four siblings and the eldest of the pack. My parents are immigrants in Sydney, Australia. When people start their lives in a new country it can be a huge risk, and there are only two scenarios you can choose from: you either go back or you make it work.

My dad has always been a bookworm. I never took notice when I was younger but he'd read personal development books about business, life, and careers. The first book that I ever read that took months to read was the *Rich Dad Poor Dad* by Robert Kiyosaki. It didn't make any sense to me at the time because I was young and never saw myself as someone who would be successful in any areas of my life.

Have you ever felt the same? Have you ever wondered if you can be a person of success? Or do you feel constantly stuck?

If these questions resonate with you, I'm going to show you a pathway and simple process that will help you adopt the framework with solid proof motivation that isn't just a hocus pocus feeling. You don't need to go crazy in taking huge leaps. All it requires is progressive steps moving forward in creating the life you deserve.

The bottom line is that you live life by your design. It doesn't matter what position or circumstances you are in—you can have an epic life. The tools, strategies, hacks, principles, and exercises listed in the coming chapters will give you that edge to thrive and propel you to the next level.

I have a saying: "Your past can never dictate your future." That means you have the opportunity of choice to be successful in any area—whether it's life, love, health, wealth, happiness, or your spiritual life. I'll help you develop key habits from proven strategies and methods that takes you from A-Z in the most simplistic approach towards your greatness.

WHEN YOU'RE NOT HAPPY INTERNALLY, IT AFFECTS YOU EXTERNALLY

If you're like me, I believe we're all good actors. We can put a mask on and no one knows what's happening within.

I always pretended to be okay internally. I didn't realize that everything I was going through in life on top of my mother's condition caused me to neglect my well-being and health. I was overweight, unhappy, and I piled up bad eating habits that got me to 220 pounds. I was overly stressed in how I manage my time at work and even before going to work I would hide myself in the car eating McDonalds sausage and egg McMuffins with large coffee. For my dinners at night, my meals wouldn't be complete until after eating chocolate chip vanilla ice cream. To be honest, these were my comfort foods. I had beliefs and negative self-talks that I wasn't good enough, not successful, and not living a fulfilling life whatsoever.

PIVOTAL POINT OF DECISION

To this day I can recall the exact experience that changed my life. I was walking up the stairs to the subway station while commuting to work, and half way up the stairs my heart began to race. I thought I was going to have a heart attack. My ankles were swollen, my legs tightened, and I thought I was going to die.

A rush of thoughts flooded my mind, thoughts of not being married, with no kids, no life, no adventures, and no family. I stood there for about five minutes in that spot, and it felt like an eternity.

I told myself, "I'm going to change my life!" I didn't know how I was going to do it, but I went for it.

I walked slowly to the train and pondered on my way to work how I would not live like this anymore. I made a conscious decision that I would be a changed person and it started with that moment.

Has there been a time in your life when "enough is enough" and you felt like giving up, wondering how to get out of the mess? Or that you're not living to your full potential yet? Or that you have achieved successes in life but not living your true purpose?

You are not alone, because I've been there many times. This time I stood up and told myself, "I don't want an ordinary life, I want an extraordinary life that is not mediocre with full of excuses."

So what happened in the process? I did a complete ninja turn around and lost 66 pounds within 16 weeks! You may be thinking, was it easy? Nope! Did you give up? Almost! Did you complain? In the beginning I did.

It seems crazy to accomplish something like this, but great things never happened in the comfort zone. I did it in the simplest strategy. If I can do it, you can too. I will show you every step of the way and it doesn't have to be just health, it could be your entire life and everything that revolves around it. You can unlock and unleash your greatness!

I FOUND MY LANE

After my transformation I knew I was made for more and it unlocked my purpose. This inspired me to create the message in this book and to write this book. I want everyone to be empowered, inspired, and have their momentum when it comes to greatness. I became really curious and wanted to understand how internally we operate, how we are influenced externally, and how we can experience breakthroughs to success.

After completing my studies as a coach and accumulating my coaching hours while coaching clients, I've noticed there are patterns and languages that people use which hold them back in the areas where they are not motivated in taking action. I believe it all derives internally that influences the external, firstly from our thoughts, behaviors, habits and action.

HOW THIS BOOK CAN UNLOCK YOUR MOTIVATION GREATNESS

Here are the six important D principles on this book to get you started:

Its starts with a DESIRE

This comes by understanding your why, your purpose, and your values in life.

It's a time to DESIGN

This comes by intentionally empowering your vision and goals.

It's about the definitive DECISION

This comes by unlocking your inner core drivers of motivation to set and achieve challenging goals.

The way to mastery is DISCIPLINE

This comes by applying the strategies, skills, and methods for progression.

Never-ending approach towards DEVELOPMENT

This comes by developing successful habits and dismantling disempowering beliefs and by replacing them with empowering beliefs.

It's the attitude that counts towards DETERMINATION

This comes by a follow through with a plan of action.

Motivation without the Hype is a book that gives you practical application from mindset into action.

You will discover the Thrive Motivation Method which is broken down into three sections:

<u>Section 1</u> is the pre-stage - Covers your internal purpose, values, principles and mindset.

<u>Section 2</u> is the during-stage - Covers your vision, goals, habits and productivity.

<u>Section 3</u> is the post-stage - Covers your follow-through and momentum.

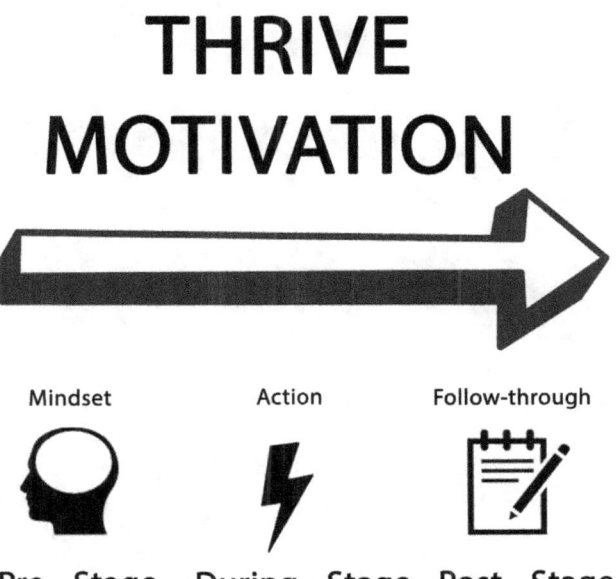

SPOILER ALERT

Firstly if you're looking for a magic wand or genie in a bottle "quick fix," there isn't any solution for this. It takes your commitment and decision to create the positive change. The goal in this book is to provide practical tips and insights in this user-friendly approach to move you into taking action. Each chapter is purposely fitted from procrastination into action and thriving forward. Here's a quote by Dwayne "the Rock" Johnson on focus: "Success at anything will come down to this: focus & effort, and we control both."

So right now you have an awesome opportunity to be the game changer of motivation to focus and make the effort. The mission of this book is to start a fire in you and inspire you to take action—it's as simple as that.

Use *Motivation without the Hype* to unleash your greatness!

PART 1:
GREATNESS STARTS WITH SELF-AWARENESS

CHAPTER 1

IT'S A NEW DAY

"Knowing your purpose gives meaning to your life"
– Rick Warren

PURPOSE

We start this book in talking about purpose because it's one of the most important keys that unlocks, unleashes, and definitely empowers you for greatness. If you've read a lot of books on personal development, purpose seems to be on the agenda all the time. I believe it with great intent that purpose sets you on course to living an epic life.

We are going to be focusing on the fundamentals of purpose that will get you moving where you want to be, rather than wishing being idle. You will create your ideal life and be ahead of the game, where others are still contemplating, confused and lost on their purpose.

Have you ever felt confused in areas what you should really do? Frustrated in life that there isn't any progress and not go anywhere? Feeling lack of purpose of what's next? Or question yourself in this circumstance?

You are not alone, I too have felt this way, and the good news is that there are insights that will inspire you to adopt a purposeful lifestyle which will open opportunities to transform your life, but also inspire others in the process.

WOMAN OF PURPOSE

Aimee Mullins is an inspiring woman of purpose. She has beaten all odds towards physicality and defined limitation as success. Aimee Mullins had a medical condition which left her with both her knees amputated at the age of one. She didn't have a choice with her situation and grew up with prosthetic legs to give her mobility. What is inspiring is that she does not see herself as disabled, and she even refuses to label it. This type of mindset creates a lot of significant possibilities.

This empowered woman had all the accolades of achievement competing in Georgetown University at NCAA track and field, then she went to the Paralympics in 1996. Years later she became a model and actress. *People Magazine* honored her as their 50 top most beautiful people in the world. No limitation was ever her challenge; she used every opportunity to make it her greatest asset.

THE FUNDAMENTALS

This remarkable story shows three fundamental phases that will help us achieve greatness where we see things in different perspectives.

Our life purpose is to grow, contribute, and give value (in different ways). Our personal growth determines the capacity in what we give.

Purpose grows within us. Purpose goes beyond goals, it's the big picture that overarches your goals and dreams. Your goals are the steps towards your purpose. When your purpose is aligned with your goals and dreams, it gives you that sense of direction resulting in peace of mind in what you're doing.

THREE FUNDAMENTAL PHASES

1. Discovery Phase – Link your purpose with your natural talent and ability

Aimee Mullins had the passion for life to challenge boundaries and developed her key skills to being the best version of herself. In areas deemed impossible, she conquered them. We are uniquely and wonderfully made with so many talents and gifts, and when you hone and discover them, you will have clear direction.

Our lives should be courageous with an empowering mindset of a can-do attitude. It's that inner self belief to experience the best life ever. I know for many or some have found it a challenge to connect their purpose and not serve their passion which could lead to internal conflict. Once we are self-aware, we have the power of choice to work towards to aligning the both which links purpose and your natural talent.

2. Action Phase – Be focused and determined

Combining focus and determination, these attributes empower your purpose to living. Knowing yourself with clarity which we will later discover can lead you to a championing mindset—it rewires your mind frame of purpose.

When your purpose is clear, your life will have meaning that brings a reason to be focused and determined to make things happen from A to Z through action. Internally you will start to think and do differently. You will start to understand how important action is that will provide results. The more you start doing, the more you start feeling and seeing the difference. You will no longer have to feel confused, lost and wondering what to do next. You'll go with the flow. You will have a purpose-driven life with confidence and clarity.

3. Continual Improvement Phase – Have a different outlook and perspective

It's all about perspective and having a different outlook that helps you shape situations and circumstances. You are not defined by it, you are in control of it. That means where you are right now will not dictate your future. You are in control of your destination and you can make the path towards greatness. When your view of outlook is positive and you see that the road ahead is hard, gloomy and difficult, this is ok. Every champion or successful person who ever lived on this earth sees things from a different perspective. What they see is the outcome, and the end in mind, which makes it more powerful because no matter what happens, they are heading that way. Circumstances and tough situations will not deter their confidence and direction.

So in order to progress and move forward all that's needed is to acknowledge the setbacks with a mindset to improve constantly. This type of attitude or work ethic to constantly improve amplifies your vision to see and achieve the bigger picture of purpose.

UNLOCKING PURPOSE

What is my purpose? I too ask myself many questions about my purpose and if I'm serving my purpose. There's a famous quote stated by Bishop TD Jakes: "Your passion will lead you right into your purpose." Hearing this can mean a lot of perspectives and different types of meanings.

Many people are not certain or unsure about their purpose. Generally it goes by getting an education, go to college, attain a degree, finding a job, climb the corporate ranks or start a business, raise a family, travel the world and retire one day, and the list goes on. It's the cycle of the mundane things of which is to eat, sleep, work and repeat. Sometimes we are dictated by our circumstances or by the surrounding of whom we associate with or the family and friends by their advice. They might say things such as, "You should do this because you are good at it."

Does this sound familiar? Well, it happened to me. I look at my dad as the kingpin salesman in real estate—the most hardworking, humbling and smart agent in his local district. Everyone knows my dad. I thought I was going to be a real estate agent too. I did give it a try and worked with my Dad. As much as I love him, it wasn't for me. I needed to find where I fit in and what I'm called to do in a way that fits my purpose and passion.

Can I say that you are in the right time? Why do I say this? Because you're on this journey unlocking your inner greatness. This is the time where you stand up to living a purposeful life with meaning and fulfilment. The question is, how?

By strengthening your self-awareness and taking responsibility. You will hear and read of these two empowering factors all the time in this book. All this takes is your absolute decision with firm self-belief to unlocking your inner genius. Now before you start going "mumbo jumbo" on me, you are a genius! I know right now you don't feel like one, let alone think like one, but you are. There is so much potential and the roaring lion in you is destined for great things!

POWER OF PURPOSE

Hearing the word "purpose" may sound like a huge thing to others. In simple terms, purpose is clear, decisive strength that compels you to create, explore, and discover. Purpose is a powerful force and knowing your purpose can provide a huge upside in your personal life that empowers your greatness!

Purpose is one of the core foundations of a fulfilling life. When there isn't any sense of purpose, this could lead to boredom, lack of direction, depression and anxiety. When there is a strong sense of purpose it creates an impact and powerful positive effect from your psychology to your physiology. This means you are in control of your circumstances, though life may throw a lot of curves, you have purpose and continue to walk in your greatness.

Why does purpose have such a positive empowering effect?

It's great for your health, it avoids all the negative chatters in your mind, and it helps with being less self-centered. It makes us feel we are part of a bigger picture outside of ourselves that allows not to focus on problems, but solutions. Purpose can enhance our self-esteem that can deal with challenges, move us closer to our goals, and elevates our self-confidence. Purpose is hope, it's a desire of optimism. Our life's purpose will always express our passion, values and gifts.

THE POWER OF VALUES

"Try not to become a man of success, but rather try to become a man of value." –Thomas Jefferson

Purpose and values is your power combo towards the self-awareness process that unleashes your greatness. They are like keys to your car, and without them, you cannot move. Values are more than a written word placed in your company statement or life statement — it is the identity that represents you, your preferences, and your importance towards it.

Values can mean a lot of different things because we all live by values and principles, so what does value mean? Put simply, it's what you believe in. Most people have a sense of what they believe in and have set values that they live by.

The influences of our values are embedded subconsciously through our family, our environment, culture, and the society we live in. It can also be part of our personality if practiced. There is a saying: "We are what our values are." Since values are beliefs, they can be empowering or disempowering. They can be limiting or uplifting. A lot of successful people have empowering values that unlock their greatness.

Values determine all our decision making. It's the principles that we stand for. If you know what your values are then you know who you are, which means it is shaped on your terms.

There are lot of people that we admire who stand up for what they believe in and stand on their values. A great example is Martin Luther King Junior who stood up for what is right according to his conviction and values during the Civil Rights Movement that led to a powerful speech "I have a dream."

When you tap into your greatness with values that are empowering, it leads you to your personal success and fulfilment. It is essential that it is lived out every day.

One of my values is integrity. This value helps me do the right thing with others whether it's my peers, family and clients. An example is throwing trash into the garbage bin at the office or in a public place.

You may experience this before, when you try to throw your rubbish into the bin and it misses, then there's rubbish around the bin. I've experienced this many times. Here's the question: What did you do with it? Leave it and walk away? Or go back to pick up the rubbish and place it in the bin? This may seem a bit odd talking about it, but for me this helped me practiced due diligence in doing the right thing.

Values gives you clarity and decision.

When you know what you stand for and what's important to you, the decision-making process becomes easier. Our values get tested all the time, particularly when things don't go our way. If for example honesty and integrity is your value, when it comes to compromise to making a white lie or a slight false information, what do you do in that instance? Lying wouldn't be your suit if you value honesty and integrity. One way or the other, we all have been tested with our values.

If you want to have feelings of fulfilment and joy, then you need to live by your highest ideals in value and standards.

WHY VALUES ARE IMPORTANT

Our values is the core of who we are and what future we want to create in experiencing. It develops our growth and maturity. How we base our decision making comes from our beliefs and values which is directed to your purpose.

For example, if your life is based on healthy living, you will not compromise in an unhealthy choice. If you value integrity and honesty, you will not cheat someone and take the shortcut because you are a person of principles and values in which you will do the right thing.

Purpose is our direction and values is our core of our decisions.

VALUE SYSTEM

The value system is an infrastructure to what greatness is about. It is where your purpose and values are connected towards an epic life.

Value of Commitment – Commitment is what you say you will do and do what you say. This is done on the basis of your decision to be accountable or accountable with someone else. This means you have commitment to your relationships, career, duties, your goals, and dreams. Having the value of commitment helps you stay on course.

Value of Honesty & Integrity – These two values are important because it sharpens your personal life for success in any avenue you go through.

Value of Courage & Self Discipline – Courage is your secret weapon to facing fears and achieving success. It's one of the power tools for greatness. Courage helps you to take a step forward without any regards that hold you back. Self-discipline is the enabler which takes action regardless of the circumstances. Self-discipline keeps you on track and gets you focus. I see self-discipline as a muscle—the more you work out, the stronger and the fitter you are in overcoming procrastination and achieving your goals.

Value of Love & Compassion – The most powerful emotion is the source of life. It's a value in what we are willing to give in exchange without the return of it. There are many perspectives, concepts and ideas of love and compassion, however through the dedication and devotion of it serves to be empowering. When values are the core of it, you will stand by it. When it is attached to your purpose, it is one of the key drivers for success.

TYPES OF VALUES

Identifying your values is key to self-awareness. It is digging deep as to what you place importance in your life. It could be, for example, that you value love, happiness, determination, family and security. There are two types of values which are both *means* and *end* values.

Means values is what you choose to experience in an emotional state you desire. For example, family, money, and success.

End values are what you want to experience. For example, happiness & fulfilment

The type of values in wanting an epic life and unlocking your greatness are the end values. These are the emotional states you want to experience.

Our true values are the end values which are the outcome. When there is clear understanding on what you truly value, then you know why you do what you do. The key to your greatness is values. We all know it's not easy as there are times where we compromise our values for the sake of pleasing others. At the end of it, we get burned by it.

So to strengthen your personal values which are wholesome, encouraging, uplifting, and positive that serve your purpose is to consciously be aware of your Top 5 values. Knowing your Top 5 as your living mantra will always be in your subconscious mind and will be your trigger point to uphold them when you are faced with compromise.

When I face my conflicting values I quickly ask myself these questions:

1. For what purpose is this?
2. Does it serve my values?
3. Can I be a person of adding value to someone's life?

It may not be exact scenario for certain situations, therefore it is always good to question yourself when facing conflicting values and find a solution of a workaround.

When it comes to your personal values, the aim now is to mirror things that you do with your values, so how do we do that?

As an example, my highest value is health, fitness, and wellness, and there are rules that I have set to meet my values and live it out every day. I commit to meditating and exercising early in the morning and having three healthy meals or snacks every day.

Here are examples of empowering values without any of the order.

Love	Strength
Faith	Accountability
Generosity	Discipline
Enthusiasm	Determination
Family	Motivation
Integrity	Optimism
Creativity	Positivity
Compassion	Adventure
Diligence	Service to others
Beauty	Reliability

What values could you see that you can potentially use or that you have now that serve your purpose and meaning?

Identifying your values gives you that edge to choose what type of states you want to be in, which can lead you to an epic life.

THE POWER OF CHOICE IS IN YOUR HANDS

Here are two quotes one by Graham Brown and Robert Kiyosaki.

"Life is about choices, some we regret, some we're proud of, some will haunt us forever. The message – We are what we chose to be."
- Graham Brown

"You and only you are responsible for your life choices and decisions."
– Robert Kiyosaki

Both quotes have resounding and similar path messages that we are the owners of our choices and it's our decisions that cause us to be where we are.

Everyone has choices and it leads to consequences that can be empowering or disempowering. Since we are humans we make decisions every single time without any thought or regard because it's in autopilot. The most important thing about direction and where you want to head in life is not to place roadblocks for yourself by blaming others or situations for poor choices. It is to be consciously aware of the choices and the patterns of your decisions.

We are creatures of habit and identifying the patterns shapes our lives. If we know what we are doing that doesn't serve us then it's time to make a positive change in our choices.

ACTION STEPS

These exercises will start to open your thinking to connecting the dots about your purpose and values. Take the opportunity right now and don't leave it for tomorrow with an excuse.

- Write out your Top 5 things you love doing.
- Write out your Top 5 what you're great and excel at.
- Write out your Top 5 values in life.
- Make list of 5 things of where you can see yourself making a difference.
- What would you do right now to implement that would change your life.

CHAPTER 2

BATTLE OF THE MINDS

"Once your mindset changes, everything on the outside will change along with it"
– Steve Maraboli

We all have our favorite restaurants we like to go to, whether it's for dining with family and friends, or going for a quick feed because of convenience.

I know there are a lot of foodies out in the world that are obsessed with trying new dishes or just love taking pictures on their smartphones to upload it into social media before eating. Nothing wrong with this at all. In fact it's great to have appreciation for the food you eat. What is intriguing I see nowadays and what you would notice is that people go to restaurants based on word of mouth, social media, and reviews. Customers, clients, or anybody who consumes products and services are huge on reviews.

I have a client and close family friend who had their business go viral on social media, hitting millions of views. This person is a renowned executive chef among the restaurant industry who served the Prime Minister of Bahrain and Sultan of Brunei and high officials, and he migrated to Sydney, Australia from the Philippines. He started out as a chef, then executive and ventured on to becoming a business owner himself.

TAKING THE LEAP

He decided with his wife to start their own burger restaurant even before hitting social media. Both started in humble beginnings. What inspired them the most is their inner why, and that is do what makes them happy and their passion for food. This led them to commence a small side hustle in catering. After they mastered catering which generated a lot of interests, they wanted to take the next step: to start up their own burger restaurant.

What was remarkable to hear was the story behind the scenes on how they grew and how successful their business became. Leading up to the burger restaurant had significant challenges which didn't discourage them. In fact, it inspired them to continue on with their dream and ambition to open.

Despite the tough competition, it was their specialty gourmet ingredients and presentation that was the difference maker. One year later, social media influencers and foodie experts took notice and tried their burgers. Their famous burger cheese dipping sauce became the "in thing" for burgers that went viral, hitting one hundred two million views and growing on Facebook, which caused huge waves of customers. Plus they were featured in different media platforms on blog articles and radio stations in Sydney, Australia.

So what won the hearts of the customers? It was the secret recipe. To this day not only am I a huge fan of their burgers, but I also love their buffalo chicken wings and ranch sauce with a tasty twist.

So how does this amazing story fit into all this? I see the secret recipe as the most important factor that is the game changer, which sets a part of the competition in any business. Just like in our lives the game changer to living an epic life is knowing that we are made for a purpose to being great. The secret sauce that we have is our greatness.

What we consistently think influences our emotions, behaviors, and actions. It may seem small, but in fact it is the major contributor toward motivation and success.

As you continue on your journey to unlocking your greatness to becoming the best version of yourself to achieving your goals, dreams, and aspiration for success, the transformation comes from the inside out. This is where you take control of your internal world so that your feelings, thoughts, and language can positively influence your outer reality.

I believe the most effective belief is to know that you are in control and that you always have a choice. We tend to allow people to choose for us because we either depend on people's acceptance or the environment you're in. You have the ability and capability to choose your own beliefs, decisions, and actions. What this really means that you understand that you are responsible for everything. We cannot control everything that happens to us but we can control the meaning of events in how to react to them.

THERE ARE FOUR EMPOWERING MINDSET STATEMENTS

Empowering Mindset 1 – The result of my actions are caused by my intention...

This means everything you do will become an outcome. When you come with a positive intention you will get a positive result through action. This is not your airy fairy positive thinking type of way. As an example, it doesn't matter how many affirmations you do if a plant needs help. You have to take action to remove the weeds around the plant, and to fertilize and water it. An empowering mindset comes with two things and that is your intention and initiation.

Empowering Mindset 2 – I see the perspectives in every situation...

It's all about a different perspective in seeing the opportunity. An empowering mindset is looking at different angles when it comes to encountering challenges. Successful people who thrive in their greatness tackle difficult tasks by remaining resourceful and calm.

Empowering Mindset 3 – I have self-belief and confidence...

To unlock and achieve your greatness is believing in yourself that you have all the resources in the world in your favor. An empowering mindset is self-worth that you know you can do anything.

Empowering Mindset 4 – There is no such thing as failure; only opportunities to grow and learn…

The ultimate empowering mindset is this statement in which we will tackle later on the chapter. Seeing a different perspective on failure can make a difference if it's viewed as feedback to learn and grow.

There is a saying: "Changing your thinking can change your results."

So when you change your thinking it replaces the negative feeling of failure into confidence for growth.

WHAT TYPE OF MINDSETS ARE WE LIVING?

The journey to transformation is by choice and not by chance, and the empowering mindset statements are influenced by the type of mindset we are living. The level to what we understand and the mindset to which you think, feel and believe, plays a part in how to live in your motivation and greatness.

Level 3 Mindset - Living in the narrative stories

Most people are living in their current stories which could be good, bad, or in between. It's the meaning and how they empower their stories. A story is anything we tell ourselves to justify not creating transformation. Here are different examples:

- I'm not a great communicator because I wasn't academic at school
- I'm poor because of my parents who couldn't care less about me
- I can't be a success because I'm such a loser at life or my life is too hard

What you tell yourself as a reason and excuse to not able to act, respond, or be happy is your story. I have done this many times not knowing that I have a mindset that is very discouraging internally. I realized this is not a quick fix, it's a learning process. We need to be aware of the stories that pop up in our minds. The story I used to say to myself was, "I can never be a success because I'm not rich, and I can't really achieve anything because you have to be smart."

The time invested in this level does not serve my personal growth. Being at this level does not support the type of your ideal life, nor does it support the vision you want. This is because your thoughts and mind are occupied with negative stories of the past, a language of excuses and the feelings of unresourcefulness and lack self-belief.

Level 2 Mindset - Knowing the why and seeking the how

At this level people know what their why is, in a way that they can change, improve, and transform their lives. People have their sights on what they envision and what it could do for them. At the same time they question the "how" part. This level is where people seek that their life, career, relationship, health, wealth or spiritual life could be better, but sit on the fence to hope, wish and wait.

This level has the potential but lacks the responsibility. It sees the future and never takes the action in the present. Whilst this level does experience levels of happiness, fulfilment, and gratitude, it may still carry a Level 3 mindset.

Level 1 Mindset - Understanding the present and knowing they are responsible

At this level people understand the moment, the season, and the time that everything is at their disposal to what happens to their lives. This comes by taking 100% complete ownership that it's entirely up to them. This type of motivation that is no hype, no gimmick and no goosebumps, but taking the self-awareness and responsibility 100% seriously.

At this stage, this type of mindset never places excuses, blaming, and justifications or complaints because they know it will stop their personal growth. It will lead their mindset as a victim and not a victor mentality. Progress is happiness and that means learning, growing, and developing gratitude that turns every situation into a positive outlook.

Gratitude and fulfilment plays a part in this level. It's a place where you become resourceful and your state of mind becomes empowering and positive.

GREAT MINDSET LEADS TO GREAT SUCCESS

"Getting rich begins with the right mindset, the right words, and the right plan" – Robert Kiyosaki

I like the quote about Robert Kiyosaki which goes beyond wealth that everything follows when you have the right mindset, right words, right plan and decisive action. Nothing is pursued unless there is self-belief with an empowering mindset.

When unlocking your greatness, nothing gets activated not until action is involved. Have you heard of the saying "knowledge is power"? I agree to a certain degree, and what I mean is knowledge is power only when knowledge is applied through action. You can be knowledgeable and fill your brain with content as much as you want, but if there isn't any progress then knowledge becomes stale.

If you want to thrive in your greatness and be zoned in to moving forward in life, then you have to execute. I'm going to be sharing with you strategies that will prepare you for unlocking the principles and universal laws that are applicable today.

"Success occurs when opportunity meets preparation" – Zig Ziglar

When you consciously prepare yourself, particularly with this book, you are intentionally setting a scene for success.

Be the person that always seeks to improve, and the only way to do that is to implement.

Let's examine what this kind of empowering mindset looks like. Your learning and growth comes by taking action and not by a perfect plan that you are waiting for.

Making a perfect plan is not enough if you only plan to just wait and procrastinate. This is the easy part that most people like to do. The hurdle and challenge is taking that plan to action.

The way you grow and learn is by going out and giving it a shot. If it does work, great! If doesn't work, that's even better.

Every setback is a setup to getting better and improving. If you can imagine a baby trying to walk, they didn't just spring up and start walking. They crawled, they stood up, they sat down, they fell, and they rose. When nature takes its course, time and time again they will walk.

As you continue to dive in more on your self-awareness, going through the process of what patterns and languages you use in your personal life gives you that advantage to strengthening your mindset.

Purpose, values, and mindset are key to your personal development that continuously builds momentum when both patterns and languages are positively used.

PATTERNS & LANGUAGES

Do you tend to feel stuck or running a negative pattern in your life that is consistent that doesn't serve or empower you? Or do you feel stagnant, like nothing is changing or transforming? Do you feel there isn't any progress? We all have set habits, behaviors, and patterns that are either negative or positive.

If you want to transform your life, unlock your greatness, shape your decisions and actions, then shifting your emotional patterns are the key. One of the fundamental tools that you can use right now is consciously and completely be aware of the choice of words that you use to describe how you feel. Instead being reactive to the situation, you are proactive by understanding the moment of that situation.

There are power words that can change your experience that can take the negative feelings and lower the intensity. What would your life be like if you could do that? How much of an impact would the quality of life be like if you could intensify a positive experience?

There are patterns that cause people to be fulfilled, happy, fit, healthy, strong, and financially abundant. There are also patterns that make people frustrated, angry, stressed, overwhelmed, depressed, sad, lonely, financially struggling, poor in health, or not having the best relationships. It's not because there is something wrong with them, it's because it's a pattern that they are running with. What is the fastest or effective way to change? It is the people who live life on their terms and take ownership that is not dictated by the current circumstances or past. The change or transformation is who we become and how we live our lives.

It is the trigger point and change is when you BE yourself.

Greatness without being fulfilled is failure. Hence if the patterns do not serve us, then there isn't any happiness.

60 Second Rule Technique

If you are experiencing anger, stress, anxiety, overwhelm or frustration, give the 60 second rule technique a try.

How the 60 second rule process works

When you start to feel the stress, whether it's angerness, frustration or overwhelm, follow these steps:

Step 1 - Let it be in the back of your mind that life is too short to be caught up in this type of emotion

Step 2 - Take a breath and breathe slowly

Step 3 - Visualize your thoughts

Step 4 - Question your thoughts and ask yourself, "Does this serve me? Does that empower me?" You will start to break the pattern of those negative thoughts.

Go through this exercise and identify which patterns that you are running right now that disempower you. What can you do right now to replace with a new pattern that empowers you?

Here's an example

Focal Point: <u>Bad Eating</u>

Current Pattern Activity:

- On weekdays after work I would binge eat on junk food, chips, and chocolate.
- Every weekend I would go on a McDonalds run and have my Big Mac Large McDonalds Value Meal.

New Pattern Activity:

- I will eat fruits and healthy snacks after work.
- I will have 6 meals a day and the last meal will be at 9pm which will be yogurt or a protein shake.

Focal Point: <u>Self Sabotage</u>

Current Pattern Activity:

- I self-sabotage myself when given an opportunity to make an impact.
- I self-sabotage into thinking that I'm not good enough even when people believe in me.

New Pattern Activity:

- I choose not to self-sabotage and I choose that I will get involve and be a person that makes a difference.
- I am good enough and more than enough that I can do things I never could do.

Now it's your turn....
Focal Point: _____
Current Pattern Activity:

- _____
- _____

New Pattern Activity:

- _____
- _____

    Recalling the words and type of language I use in the past is significantly different to how I use my words language today. If I knew what I know now, it would be a complete different narrative and in saying that I'm still happy with the journey I'm in.

    Being totally self-aware, you will notice the choice of words you use and the meaning you give it. Back then my common words were "I can't", "I don't think I can make it", "I'm not good enough", "It's too hard" and "I'm not smart enough" or "I will do it later". These types of language were embedded in my subconscious mind and every time there was an opportunity that I know I am capable of doing, these negative words would stop me from progressing. It was these words that shaped my life in creating a reality.

There is a proverb in the bible that says, "So man thinketh, so is he" or in today's lingo, "what you perceive and say, you will become." It hit me on the head and I got a light bulb moment – what you say to yourself and to others consistently is what you will experience in your life.

It's amazing how our words create a reality. I will give you an example, as this happened to me a lot in the past. Have you experienced a situation where you talk about a problem or a circumstance that hasn't even happened yet, and you stress yourself just by thinking about it? You will probably agree and the funny part is that it happens most of the time. It's because we have set ourselves into that scenario. What you speak into existence will come to pass, and this is not hocus pocus stuff.

Have you heard of this insight? "A negative mind will never give you a positive life"? Or how about "A negative vocabulary life will experience a negative life"?

What this really means if you focus constantly on struggle, pain, frustration, worthlessness, lack, anger, and disappointment this evidently is what you will experience regularly.

If it was the opposite and you focused on the positive, opportunity, resourcefulness, life, peace, happiness, and determination despite of the challenges, the experience leads you to a beautiful state.

Each one of us can experience with the attitude of gratitude.

It's impossible to get angry and frustrated if you are always grateful. The upside is that you become resourceful and the language used in your vocabulary is empowering and uplifting.

Language has an emotional intensity charge to it such as both hate and love. When you change your words, you change the way you think, feel and live.

I remember a time when I was so frustrated, as in super frustrated, that I was turning into the incredible hulk and reacted with words like:

- "Ridiculous."
- "How can this be?"
- "I just don't know now!"
- "I'm such an idiot."

- "I don't think I can do this."
- "I hate this!"

I became un-resourceful and stuck! I didn't conquer the moment—I was overtaken by overwhelm. Whenever a similar event reoccurs, my reaction is totally different.

I apply the 60-90 second rule. *I acknowledge the feeling and change my wording and see it in a different way and that I have no time to be in that state.*

So what type of language or wording would you use instead of negative words when you're in a tight spot?

Think about a time or an event that occurred that you were so upset, angry, or frustrated, and reacted with physical signs of anger. Whether you had fists in the air, hands over your head or covering your face, or you burst into tears, these signs are biochemical charges in our body when we use language that has energy.

Our language or words impacts our actions, values, and beliefs.

Here are common words used to describe some of our experiences. What words can you replace and use moving forward to unlocking your greatness?

Languages/ Feelings	Replacements
Frustrated	Concerned
Angry	Curious
Disappointed	What are the facts
Idiot	Misunderstood
Stupid	Stressed
Pissed Off	Afraid

Think of different types of scenarios and what words you could use to take it from good to great. Utilizing words that empower your experience can produce a positive influence.

Language/ Feelings	Replacements
Good	Awesome
Great	Sensational
Excited	Amazing
Like	Love
Happy	Satisfied
Ok	Fantastic

CHALLENGE ACCEPTED

Create a personal challenge for yourself in the next 10 days to only speak positive words. You can type out your positive words into your smartphone or write it down and put it in your wallet. Write out your start date and end date and be purposeful with this action.

After 10 days you will notice how much of a difference it makes in:

1. Your self-awareness
2. Change of language

It will be challenging, but believe you can do it.

After you have completed the challenge, report it in your journal.

What did you notice that was different? How did you view your language and state of mind? What type of feelings did you have staying committed? When negative words came out, how did you respond and how did it feel to know you were aware of it?

When you are self-aware with your mindset, identifying your patterns and languages unleashes your greatness. Think for a moment if these key insights weren't yet revealed—would you still have the same story and situation?

Don't let time pass you by. Take the opportunity to set yourself with success.

ACTION STEPS

This exercise will start to open your thinking to connecting the dots about your purpose and values.

- Knowing yourself a lot more, what type of mindset will you now be implementing?
- If there is one thing you have identified that you constantly say to yourself, what will you now say and do?
- Sometimes our personal stories get the best of us. What story will you tell yourself that encourages you to live an epic life?
- Identify what areas in your life that are not encouraging and what you can do right now that will make an impact in your life positively.
- What steps would you create to strengthening your mindset for success?

CHAPTER 3

GETTING INTO YOUR LANE

"Create the highest grandest vision possible for your life. Because you become what you believe"
– Oprah Winfrey

If I were to ask you to imagine what your life would look like in five to ten years from now, can you describe it to me? Can you visualize into the future? What if you can see it through? What would it look like, feel like, and be like if everything you ever wanted in life became a reality? How would that change your life? I know for a fact that asking these questions with intention does ignite a little spark in your mind and that's the power of vision.

SEE IT FROM A DIFFERENT LENS

Many people tend to see things through the lens of the impossibility, yet so many successful people have defied this because they see life through the eyes of optimism.

A noted and articulated vision came from President John F. Kennedy of his detailed speech in the Joint Session of Congress on May 25, 1961.

He said, "I believe that this nation should commit itself to achieving this goal, before this decade is out, of landing a man on the moon and returning him safely to the earth".

Can you imagine during that era and time how some people could perceive this as ridiculous and humanly impossible to accomplish this vision? However, the pursuit towards this audacious goal came with setbacks, failures, mistakes, and endless testing. On July 20, 1969, President John F. Kennedy's vision came to pass. The late Astronaut Neil Armstrong stepped on to the lunar surface and achieved the impossible by becoming the first man on the moon. The victory and commencement of this project came with a strong vision to accomplish.

Vision casting, goal setting, and strategies to action taking is the key to achieving your life's goals and unleashing your greatness to the next level. When it comes to goal setting, this mantra has always been in my mindset: "Goals are achievable when you reframe your mind—envision, plan, and execute!"

YOU HAVE TO REFRAME YOUR MIND

Most of the times even before visualizing our success, our frame of mind does not mirror our thoughts. This causes us to procrastinate which leads to leaving most people stuck in situations. So the strategy to avoid this is to let your planning be your execution, to set your goals with a frame in mind that you can do it. Acknowledging the challenges ahead working through it will give you that successful edge.

Vision and goals are paired together. Combining your purpose will only enhance your destination. It's definitely fulfilling when purpose is found and the whole perspective has shifted towards your vision.

There are 5 keys to empowering your vision that will help you turn it into reality.

1. Create your Vision
2. Initiate your Vision
3. Strategize with Clarity of your Vision

4. Take Ownership and Responsibility of your Vision
5. Execute your Vision with Passion

1. Create your Vision

The very first question we ask is, what is a vision? As stated on www.dictionary.com: "The act or power of sensing with eyes; sight. Since we have tackled what purpose is, the next step is activating your visionary senses. This means by seeing or projecting what is ahead and heading towards it with action. As individuals this step is important, as this will create the pathway you are heading to with clarity.

So how do we create a vision? Simply by asking yourself two questions.

1. Where do you want to go?
2. What do you want to achieve?

This will help you start your vision mapping and see it through for success. In the beginning of my journey when I first started this, it was a huge challenge because I made a lot of excuses, procrastinated, and still questioned myself. I wondered, "Can the things I want become a reality?"

I know for most people it is the same thinking and experiences when it comes to vision casting. This is why you need it more than ever. It's one of the reasons why successful people are really good at it because they have the intention to fulfill that vision. The more you visualize and empower your thoughts, you will realize that you are directly heading towards it.

I used to hear this saying a lot from my mother "dreaming is for free". As I grew older I realized, yes dreaming is for free and to achieve your dream, you have to pay for it. This means it takes efforts, sacrifice, hard work, and your relentless desire through action to do it and accomplish it.

So whatever your vision or goals may be, let it give you fulfilment that you are consistently visualizing and placing it in your mind and heart. Take the opportunity right now to start writing your vision. Get your journal or open your laptop and get to work.

2. Initiate Your Vision

Most often times I hear people say when it comes to casting and initiating the vision that the common thread seems to be this statements: "I'll wait for the perfect timing to start, or I'll get to it when I'm not so busy."

As true as that sounds, nothing ever gets done. Now please tell me, does this sound familiar?

If I go back to my weight loss story when I tried to lose the excess amount of body fat according to my BMI (Body Mass Index) I was considered obese. Hearing that word of obesity scares the jeepers out of me because in my own mind, I wondered how on earth I was going to get out of this condition.

During my turnaround experience what I did is after the subway incident I made a decision to change my life, I had to do something crazy that would be out of the norm and out of my comfort zone. I needed to create my own vision, get a picture, and stick it on my door so every day I purposely see this image of myself having 6 pack abs. It may sound funny to do something so outrageous, but it's what I needed to get out of the funk and do what's best in reaching my goal and vision. So it is important to make your initiation simple and effective by decluttering the negative mindset and not giving in to unreasonable excuses which can lead you into stress and procrastination.

So how do we initiate the vision? It is broken down into four simple stages. The benefits of this will give you confidence in your vision to take action.

1. *Stage 1: Focus*
    - Do not focus on your weaknesses and your past failures. See beyond that you are strong and courageous. Focus on your vision to strengthen your self-belief that empowers you to achieve.

2. *Stage 2: Write it down*
    - Be specific and write down when you will start and when you will finish.

3. *Stage 3: Setup the action plan*
    - Make a plan of realistic and achievable actions that will lead you to your vision. Aim big and go strong.

4. *Stage 4: Initiate the action*
    - Be accountable and do it consistently with absolute commitment.

3. Strategize with Clarity of your Vision

Now that you have created and started to initiate your vision, one of the key elements to enhance your vision is clarity and strategy. By being clear and concise with your vision will help you strategize to think outside of the box to achieving your vision. Total clarity gives you confidence and personal power that influences your passion into taking responsibility and ownership. The outcome of this will turn your vision to reality. This in turn gives you an advantage for progression and direction.

4. Take ownership and responsibility of your Vision.

I remember a time where my wife was my fiancée. She experienced a severe cyclone warning. It was deemed to be a powerful cyclone called Yasi in 2011 which entered in Northern Queensland, Australia, causing severe damages to the affected areas. Thankfully she avoided the storm, catching the last flight to Sydney from Cairns with her family.

It was definitely terrifying to hear the stories which led from a holiday to going back home to safety. Years have passed on and that city is still a holiday destination. What I always noticed is that storms will always pass by and not remain there forever. There will always be ray of light after the storms have passed.

So how does this story relate to my point? There will come a time where you will experience the ups and downs, the tossing, the turning, and the waves from every direction. Know this that too will also pass and will catapult you to success. Why? You will take ownership with your vision and make it your responsibility to pursue it no matter what situations come your way. You will stay on course. It's inevitable that challenges will occur, so be prepared for the storms and hold your ground. No one or anything can stop you unless you allow it to.

5. Execute your vision with passion

At the end of the day it's all about executing your vision with a powerful emotion called passion. Combining the five keys mentioned, this will lead you to empowering your vision which in return will become more real than ever. When I applied these principle keys, I started to see and experience the results. It's not easy, however, it's worth the fight and with consistency and persistency. When you start to catch a glimpse of your potential, a fire of passion becomes ignited.

When I unlocked the power of vision, it unleashed the perspective of greatness. It helped me be clearer in reaching my goals and vision. So right now take the challenge to envision your success.

HOW DO YOU SHARPEN YOUR VISION AND MAKE IT BULLET PROOF?

There are 4 ways that will propel your vision into action.

1. Simplicity is key and direction is momentum

There isn't any hocus pocus formula in what you want in life where you make a wish and it suddenly appears. Though sometimes people want a genie in a bottle that can grant their wishes.

There is a possibility that you can achieve and succeed in life by applying the power of goals. Did you know that goal setting is one of the most common habits that successful people share? Think of all the successful people you admire and aspire to be them one day. Are these the type of people that wait, wish, and hope? Or the type of people that have a compelling why, hunger, desire, determination, and purpose-driven goals? You would definitely answer the people who are determined and focused who have the attributes that would unleash and live their greatness.

Setting goals doesn't have to be hard nor does it have to be complicated. Simplicity in goals is the key and having clarity to where you want to go gives you momentum. This is where vision comes to place even before goals are set and achieved.

An example could be the captain of a ship who sets sail and sets their sight on their destination. One of the tools to ensure they are headed to the right direction is that they use to specific tool to get a good vision. This instrument is the telescope which is an optical device that can make any distant objects appear close and large depending on the scoping. Having the right coordinates and direction will ensure the destination is locked in.

So if we have our vision sighted and goals as our coordinates, then our engine to steam through is our action.

2. Goals that makes sense

We've all come to a point where we know what goals are and the benefits it brings. We're all intelligent human beings and the question we should all ask is, "Are we actually achieving our goals?"

Are we setting our daily, weekly, monthly, and yearly goals for our lives? Some say yes and some say no. I know for a fact that we have set goals but never seem to achieve them or have set them aside for later.

In the past I was filled with frustration where I procrastinated and made a lot of excuses with my lack of self-belief and confidence. This in turn led me into three categories.

1. I set goals and never achieved them.
2. I thought of the goals but never wrote them down.
3. I never attempted to take action on my goals.

Stating the three categories did not serve me well and the outcome of it all got me stuck and frustrated. It felt like I was a small mouse in a cage running on a treadmill going nowhere. Have you experienced one of these categories? I believe we have gone through something similar one way or the other and it's time for that breakthrough. By the time you have gone through this chapter you will learn how to set and achieve your goals in the most simple and effective way without any hype or airy fairy stuff.

3. Goals of excitement into action

Seasonal goals are not achievable goals. This means that most people tend to set their goals before or after the new year has passed, which we all traditionally know as a new year's resolution. It's funny to know that mostly everyone instinctively believes that new year's resolutions usually fail. I like to pose a statement that it's not failure until it's challenged. Setting goals is the easy part, achieving it through the process can be difficult. However, it's how you put it into perspective. In your journey you have to trust the process and embrace the journey.

The greatest achievement of it all is taking massive action with determination and here is the formula.

$$HABITS + CHOICES + MINDSET + TIME = GOALS$$

This formula is simple and effective when you understand that achieving goals is possible.

- ∆ You build great **habits** and set yourself for success.
- ∆ You make decisive **choices** that provides positive impact.
- ∆ You create your **mindset** that is clear, concise and empowering.
- ∆ You become more specific with your **time** to achieve it with your actions.

4. Creating value driven empowering goals without the airy fairy fluff around.

I want to show you that you can achieve your goals, dreams and aspirations in the most simplistic way. Remember simplicity is the key. The goals that you have set has to be in the present tense, that you have already achieved them. As an example you will not say, "I will earn $100k per year" or "I will weigh 22 pounds lighter." Instead you will say, "I earn $100k by December 28th" or "I weigh 22 pounds lighter." The language and tone around your words is important because your subconscious mind activates that demands stated in the present and personal tense.

The more specific you can be and when you want to achieve it must be expressed in the positive state starting with the "I" word. Goals that are written and stated will activate the law of expectation and attraction, because it will cause you to create positive beliefs increasing your energy and focus.

Empowering goals is just like a bridge. This image I want to share with you step by step how empowering goals can change your life.

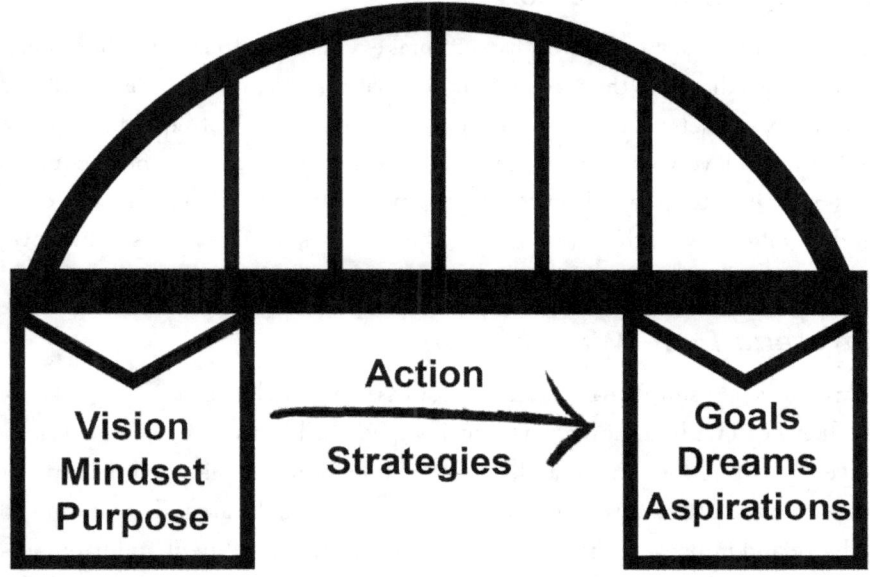

The Bridge figure 1.0

As you can see in figure 1.0, on the left hand side pillar is your vision, mindset and purpose. The bridge itself in the middle is your action and the right hand side pillar is your goals, dreams and aspirations. On the laid out bridge are the strategies you need to cross over to achieve your goals in life.

As the bridge is laid out, how do we cross over to the other side? Firstly we need to understand that its 80% mindset and 20% action. As Tony Robbins famously quotes, 80% is the psychology and 20% is the mechanics.

You can see in the example that the way to success is to have an empowering vision that is supported by the purpose and mission of the person. When setting goals, you have to visualize first what the outcome will be and experience that moment how you want to see it, feel it, and hear it.

What would it be like when achieving your goals? Every successful person visualizes their results because it draws them to their goals that gives them discipline, desire, and determination.

STRATEGIES NEEDED FOR YOUR GOALS

Strategy One – Decision

When setting your goals, you have to make a decision today. It's those clear distinctions that pave the way to your destination. Every accomplishment and intention you set starts with your decision. So decide right now that you are going to achieve your goals no matter what, that you have the inner courage to go for it without any fear. Be the top percentage of people who are clear and specific of what they want in life which tackles the five pillars of life love, health, wealth, happiness, and spiritual (meaningful) life.

Strategy Two – Write It Down

This may seem simple to do and in most cases people let their goals get stuck in their head without doing anything. I believe the key to successful goals is to have it written down in detail because subconsciously it shows your mindset you are committed to your written goal. So what are the areas do you want to achieve and improve in life? What will give you that fulfilment and happiness when accomplishing it? There is a great saying: "A goal that's not written is just a wish." If you repeat that saying over and over again it gives the truth and if you don't write out your intention, you will never get to complete your mission.

Strategy Three – Set a Date

Placing a date beside your goals gets you more effective, it places an imprint towards your subconscious mind. It gets you more committed and focused because it's right in front of you. Be clear and specific as this will inspire and motivate you to continue on your journey to succeeding your goals.

Strategy Four – Make a List

Now that you have made a decision, you have written your goals and set a deadline date, then it's time to list it out by sequence and priority. In organizing your list it has to be done in two ways.

1. Create a sequence
2. Priority

What is the order you need to complete each tasks and goals? When you have priorities in place, this will help you become productive and effective towards achieving your goals.

Strategy Five – Action

The only way you can defeat your procrastination, excuses, doubts and fears is to give it a go! Most people don't give it a go and put themselves in a situation of the *'what if'* moments. We have all gone through that phase before in wondering, *What if I did this or that?* So stop the 'what if' and allow yourself to thrive and shine out of the comfort zone. Pablo Picasso quotes it perfectly *'Action is the Foundational Key to Success.'*

Strategy Six – Do it Everyday

The strategies listed out will help you stay on track to achieving your goals. Your goals should be daily that leads to your bigger picture. You will be amazed of how far you have gone by taking daily steps forward. So here's the recap of the strategies.

1. You write your goals.
2. You set your deadline date.
3. You make a list.
4. You organize by sequence and priority.
5. You do it immediately by taking action.
6. You do it every day to get you closer to your goals.

Goals enhance your progression towards an epic life. It's part of the greatness you have. Goal setting is a learned skill and the more practice and execution you do the sharper, focused and determined you become. It's definitely a challenge to do this every day, but it's worth it at the end when you see your results. Don't let laziness be your pitfall—stay committed and just do it.

I was asked a good question in a radio interview: how do you stay motivated? I said, "Simple. These three things: my purpose, vision, and goals."

ACTION STEPS

It's time you get active and serious with your vision and goal setting. Make the effort and time in casting your vision and placing your goals that you will achieve no matter what.

- What do you need to stop doing and start doing with both your vision and goals?
- What specifically do you want to accomplish that will give you meaning and fulfilment?
- A rating out of ten, one being less significant and ten being very significant, how important is it to achieve and make your vision and goals a reality and why?
- What can you do to make your progress faster?
- What have you set aside that you know you should be working towards?

CHAPTER 4

LIVING LIFE ON PRINCIPLES

"My guiding principles in life are to be honest, genuine, thoughtful and caring"
– Prince William

We all live by principles in life whether we know it consciously or subconsciously. It is the determining factor of the basis of a decision being made or the way of life. Principles can be looked at as a way to serve a purpose or a mantra that is lived by. The sources of principles can be influenced by childhood upbringing, by association of whom you are with, or it can be taken personally to improve one's life.

Principles that are fused with beliefs and core values play an important part where it creates an internal culture from within in how you respond and live by. Have you heard of the saying "a man of principle"? It's a commonly used expression where a person faithfully follows their principle to the T that they will not compromise their beliefs or values that supports the principle.

We will discover four major insightful principles for a motivating life that will reframe your perspective in how you see things and how it can work for you if you implement one of these principles or more.

PRINCIPLE 1 – YOU ARE NOT DICTATED BY THE CURRENT CIRCUMSTANCES

Unsuccessful Person	Successful Person
Blames others of their failures	Accepts responsibility of their failures
Not bothered to learn except for TV	Takes time to learn, grow and upskill
Criticizes others and fearful of change	Compliments others and embraces the change
Negative outlook and attitude	Positive outlook and attitude
Unhealthy habits towards wellbeing	Healthy habits towards wellbeing
Doesn't care about setting goals	Focused on setting and achieving goals
Do things on their own the hard way	Associate with like-minded people
Sense of entitlement for everything	Sense of gratitude and thankfulness

Figure 2.0

Looking at the difference at a high level between both activities what a successful person and unsuccessful person do, there are both different distinction which shows significant insights of how they both operate from mindset and action.

If you read a lot of biographies and stories of how successful people operate, there are clues and similar themes that they seem to be doing. The most common attribute is that their past will never influence the future unless they allow it.

What really determines our life is the choices we make and the meaning we give it.

When you understand your self-awareness it gives you that sense of responsibility. This is why we are not dictated by current circumstances. It is the things we do today that gives us the results of tomorrow.

Universal Law Insight

The Cause & Effect: "For every cause there is an effect."

This universal law gives a lot of truth because what we do, how we decide, and the action we initiate will always become the effect. You have the power of choice and transformation. These insights takes it to the next level as this is an opportunity from a good life to an epic life. Think for a moment that everything you do today, the steps, the vision, the plan of action now becomes a reality because you have set it into motion. As an example, if we do what other successful people have done, we will eventually get the same results. Knowing the cause and effect in your life gives you the advantage that you are in control of your outcome.

Your world and what you empower is key

Your picture map, which is your blueprint, consists of your values, beliefs, and life experiences. How you create and develop your blueprint is through what you see, feel, act, smell, and taste. It's these types of senses to our world.

It's formulated into three areas

1. Beliefs – It's the meanings in which you have certainty of.
2. Values – It's what you stand for and the emotions experienced on a daily basis.
3. Life Experience – What has occurred from past to present.

Studies show that are roughly two million or more bits of information we process every day, now that's a lot of information to bear but there is a system. This is called the filtering system where it consistently deletes, distort, and generalize every event and what it means. How our minds decides is through what we filter in our beliefs. We are all unique and the meanings we give are very different. When two people both say, "That was an awesome intense movie," the meaning from each person could be different. Person A could mean that the movie is very violent. Person B could mean that the movie had intense drama scenes.

The filters in our mind delete what is irrelevant, distort it to fit in what we experience, and generalizes what we have experienced before. So for example, say there is a project that was assigned to you that was completely new. What type of filtering system are you using to decide what to do about this event? You could be deleting your abilities to fulfill this new project.

What events would be needed to distort to giving you stress? Maybe you're generalizing the information and doubting that this project can be done. What if this was turned around? Where have you had supporting experiences where you had success in the past in completing and delivering your projects? What would your filters be like?

I remember in my past where I was overweight. My belief system was that I had big bones and that it was in my genes to get fat easily. It was an excuse I chose to not do anything to improve my health. So what type of filtering system would I be giving? Not a good one.

So the key to empowering my blueprint in this example is to change it. It is by installing and empowering my filtering system. I replace the words "I can't" into "I can."

What I did to transform my body was this: I purchased a health men's magazine and cut out the six pack abs model and replace his head with mine. I connected my beliefs with others that if they can transform their lives I can too.

PRINCIPLE 2 – YOU ARE THE ARCHITECT OF YOUR LIFE AND THAT MEANS 100% RESPONSIBILITY

When I hear about the word responsibility all I think about is a position given in titles and accountability it brings. In the past I didn't understand the power of responsibility. All I knew back then was to go with the flow in life and not steer the direction to where I want to go, and to let the storms of my life direct me.

This may be true for others that responsibility can be challenging because other people are used to being dictated by circumstances or by their peers' or family's opinions. They never seem to take a stand what they want to do and do it for themselves, and that makes them feel they are in control and empowered by choices of their destiny.

I believe the key to breakthrough is to be the victor and not the victim, and that responsibility is anchored as a super hero. Every hero in their DNA comes with responsibility they know it's their duty to protect themselves and others from harm when a villain is uprising to do some damage. We all know that in most movies every super hero always wins.

This type of example is what I see when we are responsible and take responsibility as it brings out your identity of ownership and authority. Think about this example for a moment: you are a superhero that has responsibility for greater good. Wouldn't it feel awesome? Knowing you are the person in charge, knowing that your decisions come with confidence and that you know your absolute purpose and calling?

This is the power of responsibility, that you are the victor. You don't blame, make excuses, justify, and go in self-pity mode. You are the complete opposite. You know that decisions shape your destiny and it is your choices that positively impact your life for the better.

Responsibility holds us accountable

Remember the law of cause and effect. It's what we do and how we respond.

The challenge part for everyone is to embrace the concept. This is due to people questioning that things happen without knowing, or that is out of their control and can't be prevented. The best way is to acknowledge it and not dwell in it and is to take this concept as a learning experience. It's how you choose to respond.

You are the architect of your life

It is empowering to know that you can design your ideal life and that you can lead right into it. It's that responsibility factor to ensure that it's chartered to that course.

Taking 100% responsibility means that you don't look to the left or right to find excuses that didn't work or say that it was their fault and not yours. It's all about how you respond and what you do afterwards. We know life will throw a lot of twists and turns your way and that shouldn't stop you from wanting an epic life.

I know for me in the past I hated the responsibility. This is because it was easy to blame others and not myself. I used to blame my parents a lot internally as to why my circumstances were different. I used to say, "If my parents did this then my life would be different."

I made it toxic for myself. I couldn't seem to enjoy my life to the fullest and take the ownership that I can live a different positive direction.

Have you experienced where the person not taking responsibility for their actions doesn't seem to break free? Hence why as you learn this principle you'll see how language and mindset play an important factor. Instead of the having a powerless feeling we can say, "I acknowledged this has happened. I don't like it and I'm determined and willingly to find a different solution."

What about this commonly-used words, "Why me?" This can be discouraging at times when we use these words. Since we know now how to replace the wording we can say, "It's me because I'm the person with all the resources I need to deal with it head on."

You are the decision maker to your life and you have everything in your ability to make it happen and create that ideal life.

Remember transformation does not happen by luck, it

> **Number 1 - <u>Commit</u> to play 100% that you create the transformation right now. Not tomorrow, not next week or year.**
>
> **Number 2 – <u>Believe</u> that you can transform. You need to tap into your inner genius that you have all the resources within you, and the greatness from within you. Create the life on your terms and be the architect of your ideal life.**

happens by decisive choices. No one is responsible for you, only you are when it comes to outcomes and results. You are responsible in how you respond whether you choose to be sad, frustrated, angry, upset, happy, or empowered. The past events that may have happened to you, whether it was at school, friends, bullies, colleagues at work, family or parents can't prevent you from living an epic life.

If you choose responsibility in your life, your perspective in how you see things will be different. So how do we do it?

Number 1 - **Commit** to play 100% that you create the transformation right now. Not tomorrow, not next week or year.

Number 2 – **Believe** that you can transform. You need to tap into your inner genius that you have all the resources within you, and the greatness from within you. Create the life on your terms and be the architect of your ideal life.

Universal Law Insight

Law of responsibility - We are each responsible for everything in our lives.

This universal law tells us that when we are responsible it empowers our decisions, it opens to be receptive to learning lessons during the process as well as making internal and external changes in our current situations.

Owning up is your spark plug for success.

I believe that responsibility is your key ignition for success. It's where you take initiative and know that the actions you take will result an outcome.

PRINCIPLE 3 - WHAT YOU SET AND FOCUS ON IS THE RESULT IN WHAT YOU GET IN RETURN

"Always remember your focus determines your reality."

- George Lucas

The principles so far have highlighted your internal blueprint and the perspective about responsibility has provided a lot of impact in taking the challenge in unleashing your greatness.

A complete focused and zone-in approach towards anything in life can reap a lot of rewards. It's where determination and drive comes from. Nothing else matters when you are completely focused. There have been many articles, books, courses about focus and the principle mentioned confirms it all.

What you really focus on is what you are going to get.
I remember an episode I watched by Dr Mehmet Oz, where Tony Robbins was the guest and spoke to the audience. He told everyone to close their eyes and only think about the color brown. Within seconds they opened their eyes to find out that the audience was looking for brown items. It deleted every color around it and made it relevant to what it is set to focus.

This exercise demonstrates how are our minds operate. It searches and focuses on what you have set it to focus on.

Focus allows us to concentrate on what we are doing and ignore every outside noise. If we channel on the right empowering things, the more we become focused will lead to more success. This type of focus is not only for self-help, but for business, leadership, career, sports, and academics.

Your energy is fueled by the focus you place and it can be negative or positive.

When you focus on how hard life is, how frustrated you are all the time, how annoying things can be for you, and that you can never win or accomplish, these will be the results.

When you focus on the positive where there is passion, purpose, fulfilment, and love, it's these wonderful experiences that you will get.

Law of Focus

We move forward to what we focus on.

This law also adds on to say that what you think about expands. This means your mindset expands and leads you to that direction.

I'm always amazed when I see elderly people who are in their sixties and seventies still strong and fit in the gym. I couldn't believe my eyes so I asked them how old they were, in a conversation of course. What I noticed is that they are optimistic and have healthy strong minds.

On the other side of the coin I have seen other elderly people who are frail, weak, and seem to not enjoy life as before. This could be many reasons and most of the times it's the praises of their past and how they live in their negative stories.

There is a powerful search tool that we use called Google. Statistics mentions that there are 40,000 search queries every second on average which is translated to over 3.5 billion searches per day. It's mind-blowing to know that the whole world uses Google, that every search word produces a result.

The same principle is what we focus on will determine the result we are going to get.

I have come to realize that it all comes to this, it's passion and determination that brings out the internal hunger:

PASSION + DETERMINATION = HUNGER.

It's the hunger that formulates that zoned-in FOCUS.

I'm a firm believer that everyone that unlocks their greatness unleashes their hunger with an empowering focus.

Be a hungry lion

Hunger takes out every excuse and takes every challenge to the next level to being more fit, more efficient, more effective, more accurate, stronger physically, stronger mentally, and gives you the courage to achieve the best results.

When you shift your focus, you may not see the immediate result and that's ok. Just stay consistent and persistent.

As an example, you cannot have a flat stomach or a chiseled abs in one day, as it takes time. What you can do right now is focus what you want. Be that hungry lion, be the lion who is fearless! Remember, champions are those who do not make excuses. They let their fighting do the talking. That means action.

I believe to achieve greatness in our personal lives we all need that type of hunger to press on and not give up on what we want in life.

I was sitting in a workshop with JT Foxx, wealth coach and he profoundly said, "If we don't have a bigger hunger for success, you will never get there."

PRINCIPLE 4 – LET GO OF THE OLD AND ALLOW THE NEW

In life, time will always progress. It never stops, it's constantly ticking, and the thing about time is that we can never turn back. What we do now with time matters. If we don't stop with self-awareness, 5 years will pass by quickly.

There are two words I want to point out in relating to time in Greek which is Kronos and Kairos. Kronos is the measure of time which is minutes and seconds. On the other hand Kairos means an appointed time, it is an opportunity moment of impact within that time. I believe you are at this Kairos time and it's your decision to unlock your greatness for success. Personal growth comes with letting go of the past, things you did that have stopped you and embracing the unknown to the new. What you do with your time is up to you, but you have an opportunity to turn things around in your favor and live life on your terms.

If you study every successful person, they all have a story, but it is a new profound positive story that they create that leads them to abundance. They understand how important time is and that the only way to experience fulfilment is taking action. Think about all the innovators in the world. They didn't sit down on their ideas wait till cows come home. It took action from a test product, refining the product, and launching the product and improving the product ongoing. It's the same approach we need to take. It may not be perfect in the beginning to what we envision, but you will get better to achieving your dreams, goals and aspirations.

It's all about growth and development

I remember I did a twitter rant and posted it on social media about what I thought on personal development. I said, "Personal growth is not all about learning new information but it is unlearning old limitations and beliefs. This inspires transformation into empowering possibilities."

Socrates said, "The secret of change is to focus all of your energy, not on fighting the old but on building the new."

It's your time to shine and build on the new! Yesterday can be a learning past for the present to create a successful path for the future.

Playing it safe and stuck in the comfort zone won't get you anywhere. Great things happens when you're out of the comfort zone.

There is a classic movie called the 10 Commandments starring Charles Heston who also starred in Ben Hur. This is not going through a religious route but the story has a lot resonance in a way the narrative has been told.

In the movie of the 10 Commandments which the main character is Moses depicted in the bible. His sole purpose was to rescue his people from slavery and lead them to the promised land to which God has promised them. There was a particular scene in the movie where it build into the highest suspense when the Israelites came with such joy being released by the Pharaoh only to find out they are being chased down the line so that the Israelites would return as slaves. Frightened and scared that the Israelites might return to slavery, they saw an enormous obstacle that in the eyes of man was impossible to cross and reach: the Red Sea. Just picture yourself for a moment being in that scene being stuck, chased, and potentially being killed for leaving Egypt, only to have the Red Sea between you and the Promised Land.

Moses, chosen by God, raises his staff and the waters part. This was a miracle to the Israelites, but would they step forward? Would they trust in their God and be prepared to let go of their past and embrace the uncertainty of a brighter future? The Israelites walked through the Red Sea with victory.

So how does this story resonate with us? There are choices that we make. Are you ready to cross over? Are you ready to step forward to the unknown that is unfamiliar to being familiar? Are you prepared to say yes to yourself for the uncertainty to the certainty?

I believe it's your time now to live your principles that supports your greatness with an empowering motivation. Don't delay the process and embrace of who you are and what you're capable of because you are truly destined for greatness. So start applying the principles and live out the best life ever.

ACTION STEPS

Living your life that is congruent with your principles is your internal valuable asset. Not only do you stand on your principles, but you live them by your actions.

- Write out your Top 5 Principles.
- After going through a personal evaluation, what new principles will you live by?
- Out of the principles mentioned, what would you take on board and why?
- Have there been any situations where you have lost your focus? What do you need to do to get it back?
- What do you need to let go of and what do you need to embrace right now?

PART 2:
GREATNESS IS ALL ABOUT EXCELLENCE

CHAPTER 5

BRING IN THE STANDARDS

"We are what we repeatedly do. Excellence then is not an act, but a habit"

– Aristotle

CHANGE YOUR HABITS, YOU CHANGE YOUR LIFE

Changing your habits can change your life dramatically. I remember listening to a motivational audio and it was Walter Bond, international speaker and former NBA player, speaking on the winner's mindset.

Two key words that he specifically mentioned that really resonated within me:

1. Habits
2. Rituals

In order to work on your game and give it your absolute best is to empower your mentality of not giving up to build strength on your mindset, execute and dominate. How do we do that?

It's all about recognizing your current habits, identify what habits bring you down that hinders your success, and then replacing it with the good that attaches with consistency till it becomes a ritual.

> **It's all about recognizing your current habits, identify what habits bring you down that hinders your success, and then replacing it with the good that attaches with consistency till it becomes a ritual.**

Having your personal goals and vision in place gives you that head start, therefore it takes your momentum further into having solid habits that is crucial to your greatness. The key difference is the type of habits that you choose that will lead you to success. Your habits will always determine your outcome regardless where you are right now in life.

Successful people have successful habits and their challenges will not waver them of their pursuit for an epic life. So it all comes down to choices in which life you want. Our outcomes and end goal don't just happen, they are results of our decisions and how we respond to act.

What is a habit? In simple terms, it is what you do repeatedly that influences your behavior that becomes automatic. The positive news is that you can change your habits into your favor. Say for example that your health is at your highest priority, that you're wanting to feel great physically, emotionally, and mentally by having more energy and vitality. There are certain traits and habits that are required to do so to accomplish this. See yourself already attaining your new habit and by having your vision and goals prepared only increases your motivation to act.

If you're wanting to improve your financial future, it takes your decision and habits to make it happen. If the desire and goal is to experience true abundance in wealth, there are certain money-making habits that are needed.

Obsession in a positive state that is grouped together with consistency will transition you into where you want to be in your financial future.

Are you making adjustments to your expenses and budget? Are you paying yourself first? Saving and investing 10 percent of your income? Are you constantly tracking where your money goes? In most cases people tend to be inconsistent in their habits and goals, not until a decision is made to build a consistent habit and that responsibility is taken on board owning the entire results.

GOOD HABIT OR BAD HABIT? IT'S OUR CHOICE AT THE END

We all have habits and it can go both ways. We can have good habits or bad habits and these two can determine your progress in where you are going in life. I remember a time where my wife was raving about this clip she saw on Facebook relating to heart attacks and it was the former US President Bill Clinton. Did you know he is a complete Vegan? It was a shock to me because most Americans I know love their meat, however former President Bill Clinton has changed his nutrition completely from eating burgers and fries into eating vegetables and greens. Heart attacks are normally influenced by poor health choices and how the body is treated. I believe your health is super important.

As they say, "Health is your wealth," and building great habits from the start can bring outstanding long-term benefits. I was even surprised that this lady on social media was seventy years old and look so much younger. I couldn't believe my eyes. One of her secrets to looking and feeling youthful is that she stopped eating sugar completely in her forties. Wow! No more chocolates, ice cream, and all that sugar you store in your body. It really does take discipline and foreseeing the benefits in the long run.

A lot of my clients have asked me how long it takes to build great habits. This is a good question and it all depends on the recipient. To develop a habit and behavior is determined by the repeated pattern in which your emotional state connects with on your decision to act a new habit.

Every bad and good habit has its consequences. If you do things in a certain way, it will bring a predictable result in that manner. When there's negative habits that don't uplift you, it will create a negative result. In turn if there are successful habits, it will create positive outcomes.

FIRST THINGS FIRST

As we all know the power of self-awareness is to step back and evaluate your life. The most common challenge that we face is time. We never seem to make the effort to stop and think what we actually do that either empowers us or leaves us in the mundane things of life.

As you read this take the time right now to really ponder and think through your habits. To get started, what has always worked for me is the (H.C.E) Habit Checkpoint Evaluation that is simply the pillars of life. Identify your current habits from your personal life, health, wealth, relationship, career and spiritual life. Going through the discovery is to find what you need to replace and how you can empower your new habit.

ELIMINATION OF BAD HABITS IS THE WAY TO WIN

It is said that great habits are hard to form but easy to live with. Bad habits are easy to form but hard to live with.

Replacing a bad habit with a successful habit is to do it by repetition. You are what you think as well as what you do in your consistent habits. Habits are learned and can be unlearned.

There is a Three Step Method towards an empowered habit.

Method 1 > Eliminate bad habits

Method 2 > Create successful habits

Method 3 > Modelling successful people's habits

METHOD ONE: Eliminate bad habits
When you hear the word eliminate, our tendencies is to have that little doubt which spurs questions 'can bad habits ever be eliminated?' I would say yes, if repeated with a good habit repetitively overtime. Make the effort and go all-in.

Here's the practical side for method one.

1. Identify your triggers

As you self-evaluate and list out all of your habits, pinpoint what they are with who, when, where and what. Here's a list of scenarios that will get your mind going.

> What emotions at any given time tend to provoke your worst habits such as stress, frustration, anger, fatigue, anxiety, boredom etc.?
>
> When experiencing such emotions what are you doing, whom are you with, where are you?
>
> What are your normal routines? What do you normally say when you wake up? How do you feel when thinking about certain things, what type of mood are you in regularly?
>
> What time do you normally snack or fall into bandwagon of eating junk food?
>
> What bad habits pop-up in your mind and in your activities?

It may sound like it's in your face, and in fact, these questions alone can give you significant awareness to do something about it. I want to encourage you to not delay this process. I would suggest to stop right now, get your notebook and go through these methods. You will feel much better you did.

2. Take action of your triggers

Next step is to identify your triggers and make sure there's a follow-through mechanism in your action. So, for example, if you have a poor diet and you know that the food you are consuming is not giving the results you need for a healthier lifestyle, then its judgement day on your fridge. "Take out the junk!"

This means you need to clean out the fridge and cabinets and replace it with the good healthy meals and groceries. If your habit runs on sweets snacks, replace them with a healthier protein bar or dark chocolate. If you know that there are certain situations that give you stress, overwhelm and procrastination, then you must decide to take action. Turn it around for your success.

3. Ease into it

Sometimes going into a new habit cold turkey can be good and bad for others. So the best approach towards habits is to ease right into it with a purpose and goal in mind. When circumstances and mistakes happens when it comes to your new habit never let it discourage you, keep going till its second nature to you. As Jim Rohn says, "Motivation is what gets you started. Habit is what keeps you going."

METHOD TWO: Create Successful Habits

Your focus and intention will initiate your inner motives to creating successful habits. After eliminating your bad habits, the next phase is to replace them with great habits for success.

Here's the practical side of method two:

1. Decide right now

Decisions goes both ways. We all know that if decisions are made later it will never happen. I have been on that road many times. It will lead you to just throw in the towel. Make a decision for successful habits in your life that you know that will inspire you to live an epic life.

2. Don't make any excuses and say you'll do it next time

Stick to your guns and play it out 100%. The resistance to breaking into a new habit will be challenging, but it will be rewarding when you go through the journey. If one of your goals is to get up in the morning early to either read, listen to inspiring messages, or to exercise, don't be stuck in bed and say I'll do it tomorrow or even hit the snooze button.

A quick tip is have your smartphone away from where you are, so it forces you to get out of bed. Soon as your feet touches the floor, you're half way there to accomplishing goal to starting your day out of bed. Try it because it's worth the effort and you will feel great you did.

Repetition is the secret weapon to your discipline which is the key, so get right up till its automatic in your system.

3. Say empowering words to your life and visualize that you are already doing your habit

Saying and visualizing your habit is crucial to getting you to staying on track. The more consistent you become and the more you are committed to your actions, it creates that empowering psychology of your new behavior, being accepted by your subconscious mind thus being automatic.

4. Keep going and reward yourself

When you feel you are uncomfortable with your new habit, keep on going, it means that it's working. There will be times where it gets real challenging to revert back to the old habits, but the more you keep at your new habit, the easier and automatically it will become. It's important to reward yourself when your habit becomes established. It helps your mindset and you feel amazing that you have done it when you thought it was impossible.

5. Set yourself for success

We all know that Rome wasn't built in a day, however Rome's progression still continued, with much preparation, patience, and execution until the city was built. When you consciously with effort prepare and work on your habits to be the better version of yourself, you will notice the difference from within and how you respond, react, and are consistently proactive in your new habits. See it through to the future of how having new habits can change your life and embrace the process. Go into preparation, stay patient and execute.

6. Have an accountability buddy

Accountability that is grouped together into persistence, patience, and perseverance will help you and elevate your habits for success. Surrounding yourself with an accountability buddy will encourage you to continue on your journey, whether your goals is to have better habits in your relationship, career, business and personal life. Don't be afraid to share, going together as a team will help you continue your journey towards great habits. In terms of environment, culture, and accountability we will go in depth in the chapters to come.

METHOD THREE: *Modelling successful people's habits*

One of the causes of delays, success, and people giving up along the way towards what they want in life is people tend to do things on their own. They like to reinvent the wheel when the wheel has already been built. This type of mindset will only cause frustration. I have experienced this situation many times and it has not served me well. My ego played a huge part on this and I needed to change.

I have experienced this frustration until I wanted to work smart and not hard at the wrong things. I realized I needed to do something different and do things right and properly. Take note on the word properly.

I started weight training at the age of 18. I turned from a very skinny guy to an overweight guy. How does that happen? I relied on second information of others who are in the gym that are also ego lifters. I did things own my own. I never sought out any professionals, coaches, and experts in the industry. The only time I got my body transformation is I kicked out my pride and sought help and guidance.

So the question we need to ask is, why reinvent the wheel if the process in getting success is already laid out? Why go through the journey with frustration where there are methods that have been tested and experienced? Why go alone when you know others have paved the way for success?

As truthful as this sounds it's got significant substance where Tony Robbins says, "Success leaves clues." You follow the same process and formula, you will get the same results.

YOUR GAME PLAN FOR SUCCESSFUL HABITS

I'm a firm believer when a blueprint is followed, you will get the exact design to what is planned out. Just like a house, if you build the right specifications from the architect design, you'll get a beautiful built home.

The habits of highly effective people that take their greatness to higher levels for success is their understanding of successful habits. Results may not be immediate and not happen first hand and straight away but it will eventually show up.

Here are the most common traits that are the focal point to living an epic life:

Daily goal setting

Results-driven

People-oriented

Health-oriented

Personal development skills

Self-discipline

DEVELOP AN EFFECTIVE WAY FOR HABITS

Developing great habits with intention with the right focus will make you effective. A lot of sources says it takes at least 21 days to break and form a new pattern of habit. However, the amount of days it will take should not be the concern. The aim is to get started.

There are different ways of methods and days to break and form a habit. What we need to have is the sense of urgency. Never wait—you must start now.

Take the (G.H.C) Great Habit Challenge to develop great habits to help you become the best version of yourself.

Great Habit Challenge

- Waking up early in the morning and exercise.
- Planning your day before the day starts and be productive.
- Listening to podcasts and give yourself personal growth.
- Be on time with appointments and be punctual and consistent.
- Practice gratitude and daily reflection.
- Strive for excellence and manage money wisely.

You can be as creative as you want to be, but this is a great start to developing your empowering successful habits. Practicing with repetition will assist you to develop great habits.

ACTION STEPS

After going through the insights, methods and strategies of habits, it's time you let your successful habits accelerate your greatness so you can live an epic life that thrives and definitely shines.

- Write out your top 5 bad habits
- What triggers your bad habits and what do you need to do to replace it?
- What personal habits would you need to have to become successful?
- Write out two insights you have learned that has resonated with you
- Select which challenge would you do in the (G.H.C) Great Habit Challenge

CHAPTER 6

DEVELOP A HYBRID SYSTEM

"Productivity is never accident. It is always the result of commitment to excellence, intelligent planning and focused effort."
– Paul J Meyer

One of the most important parts to unleashing your greatness particularly in the area of excellence is being a superstar of productivity. Is it easy? No. Is it hard? No. Is it achievable? Yes. Will it take time and effort? Yes. Is it fulfilling to get things done? Absolutely yes!

Being productive is more than just flipping the switch, it is influenced by your vision and goals through action. What you will learn are the details of productivity tips and insights to help you get more productivity out of your day with less time involved. One of the most common phrases spoken is, "I'm too busy." Sometimes this means being busy without being productive. Does it sound familiar?

I placed myself in that situation until I was serious about creating and wanting an epic life which requires intention and effort. So tell yourself right now that it's time to activate your power of productivity. What you will get are the secret productivity hacks to be smart and achieve things that are of high value in return. If we remove of the technical jargon that's running in our head and make it simple, you will actually become highly productive. The aim and approach is to be a high performer when it comes to productivity than a busy bee.

THE THRIVING WAY TO BE PRODUCTIVE

Being productive consistently is challenging for a lot of people and whilst for others it can be a breeze. This is because it's all about *habits* and seeing the importance of *getting things done* immediately.

In most cases we can fall into a trap and procrastinate all day long when we attempt to be more proactive in our approaches. What we tend to do is be reactive and force ourselves to do a task that may not be of quality. The thriving way to productivity is a simple approach and that is systematic, effective, and less time wasting.

Everyone has their own version of what productivity means. Just search in Google and you will have a ton of blogs, articles, and programs all about productivity listed. Knowledge is great and the only way it becomes power is when it's applied. In this chapter there are two components in which it has eight key points to understanding how the thriving way can lead you to more productivity. Here are the two distinctions between productive and busy.

Being Productive = Outcomes & Results

Being Busy = Stress & Overwhelm

To get started, what is productivity? On www.dictionary.com it states, "The quality, state, or fact of being able to generate, create, enhance, or bring forth goods and services." I like the words "bring forth" because what it means is to bring it forward to generate an output to what you put in. So in simple terms, productivity means what you put in is what you will get. It's the same as the universal law of Cause & Effect.

PRODUCTIVITY INSIGHT

Your outcome is the result of your input. Work smarter not harder—stay productive, not busy.

Outcome focus

Your outcome is driven by your input. If you decide to get things done, you will get the result.

So the question we need to ask ourselves is, what is your why? Understanding and knowing your why is one of the key drivers to get you moving forward and start achieving.

There are a lot of possible scenarios of your why.

- You want to be a better person
- You want to have an awesome career or business
- You want to have wonderful fulfilling relationships
- You want to have great health
- You want to have an amazing family and always be present

All these whys are great motivators that help you be the best version of yourself. It's time you decide how you picture your results and move toward them. Your productivity is your opportunity to be a high achiever.

PROVIDE THE INPUTS

Nothing happens if you don't do anything. Twiddling your thumbs will not get you to your destination. Your contribution to adding your effort and deciding to do something with your time effectively will be the difference maker. To be smart in your approach and strategize efficiently will evidently bring maximum results.

Productivity in itself involves energy, time, and attention management. With the right resources at your disposal, you are one step closer to conquering your day.

PUTTING THEM TOGETHER

Now it may sound great so far reading the content, but how do we put this all together? Good question.

Say for example you are a Marketing Consultant specializing in web development and your business can create 10 websites including Facebook ads within 10 days.

The Outcome Goal – 10 websites including 10 Facebook ads each

The Input towards the Goal – 10 days

So how would you increase your productivity?

- You can double up by pumping 20 of your outcomes within 10 days
- You can do 10 of your outcomes within 5 days
- You can do both 20 outcomes within 5 days

You may look at this and say, "Wow, I can do this." In fact, you can. All it requires is prioritization, good planning, and other factors using productivity strategies using resourcing techniques. When you are self-aware of your capabilities and take responsibility, it takes you to a whole different level towards how you can be more productive.

PRODUCTIVITY INSIGHTS

Your ways to win is the following: strategic planning, scheduling, reviewing, setting achievable goals, developing great habits.

Just do it

Don't get held back because you don't know where to start—just start. Put out a simple checklist and identify your top three absolute items you need to complete, and use this technique as starters for now. It doesn't matter what tools, apps, or methods you use, just start your day to win and execute. Be proactive and really conquer your day by setting important goals and tasks. Decipher by utilizing how to prioritize and focus what gives you the maximum return in value.

The productivity insights will show you how successful people are productive and effective in getting things done. There are 12 strategies that successful people do that leads them to win every day.

STRATEGY #1. Execute what works that provides maximum output

Highly productive people are go getters. They base their actions towards systems and processes meaning rituals/habits. Streamlining the current process and making it more efficient will provide maximum output.

STRATEGY #2. Finding ways to get better

Highly productive people are constantly reviewing the good and the bad, the positive and the negative when it comes to execution. There will be times of challenges, issues and problems. Successful people are self-aware to evaluate, adapt, evolve, and constantly refine.

STRATEGY #3. Great planners

Margaret Thatcher said, "Plan your work for today and every day, then work your plan." Basing what works and what needs improving helps their planning to be efficient in time management as well as effective in their productivity. Highly productive people are those who take their vision into reality by allowing their habits take a step forward into action.

PRODUCTIVITY INSIGHTS

Be Self Aware – Be realistic in your approach and strategic in your planning

STRATEGY #4. Solution focused and understanding the seasons

Highly productive people understand there will always be seasons whether it's summer, rainy, or winter. The game plan is preparation. Our life's situations and obstacles are inevitable. Successful people are not wavered or conditioned to go with the motions. They can still continue their endeavor because what they have set is important to them. So we need to model the same attitude and be solution-focused to continue on.

STRATEGY #5. Take notes

Highly productive people are note takers. When there is an innovative idea, or something that springs to mind that solves a problem or provides amazing value, successful people immediately note it down. Even if they don't have a notebook, smart phone devices are also utilized. We should never put a limitation to what we are capable of. We humans like to be lazy and take the easy route. We think we'll remember something without writing it down, but then we often forget it. Make the habit to write ideas or important details down or note them on your smart phone.

STRATEGY #6. Prioritization is crucial

Highly productive people are great planners because they know what to prioritize and delegate, and they can find available resources. Successful people have systems in placed that provide significant value in what they do best. The Pareto Principle which is the 80/20 rule should be applied when tasks are in progress for completion. This is means focus on the 20% that will give you 80% of your success.

PRODUCTIVITY INSIGHTS

Ditch the smartphone – Schedule your time to go on Facebook avoid getting stuck on the newsfeed

STRATEGY #7. Only focus one thing and follow-through

Highly productive people know how to prioritize which doesn't involved in multi-tasking. It's that single point of focus that gives maximum results without distractions or procrastination. Multi-tasking can drain your brain power and energy, which is not ideal if you want things done efficiently.

STRATEGY #8. Setting standards

Highly productive people do not compromise when important tasks are at hand. Placing standards brings out quality. Allocating time, energy and focus produces success. Successful people know their limits and want to ensure that proper investment of time is given.

STRATEGY #9. Systemize and delegate

Highly productive people understand that having systems in place can streamline any process they do. When it comes to productivity, successful people know how to unlock their resources whether it's through smart applications, systems, resources, or delegation.

PRODUCTIVITY INSIGHTS

Be agile - Break down into smaller goals that can be worked within a 1 week sprint

STRATEGY #10. Quality Questions = Quality answers

Highly productive people are always asking quality questions to create curiosity to getting quality answers.

Questions such as:

- What can I do to get better?
- What are the smart ways to being productive?

- What is my current process I can shave off that are lesser steps in doing?
- What are the latest tools that can assist my game plan?

STRATEGY #11. Turn good into great habits

Highly successful people build habits to get them closer to their goals, dreams, and aspirations. Take the challenge to turn your bad habits into great habits. Be constantly aware to do things that improve your internal value such as reading, exercising, and networking with like-minded people. Hone in great relationships around you.

STRATEGY #12. Constant and never-ending improvement

As the famous quote stated by Benjamin Franklin says: *"Without continual growth and progress, such words as improvement, achievement, and success have no meaning."*

Highly productive people are always constantly improving with the intent to always get better. It should be our goal to make improvements and better our lives to be efficient and do things we love.

PRODUCTIVITY INSIGHTS

Skip social media first and start your important tasks before anything else

Suit up for success with intention

There is a famous quote by Tim Ferris, the Author of *The Four Hour Work Week*: "Focus on being productive instead of busy." This has a lot of truth in it because most of the time we like to be busy just to be busy. The productivity has not been considered when we are busy because the level of activities are not focused on returned value. For example it is work or business related, answering all emails and neglecting other important meetings to follow through can be a huge challenge and the solution around this is to prioritize the workload effectively.

Most people have their 'to do list' in their head, however, almost fifty percent of the time it never gets written down. This can be time consuming and already you have lost productive time that gives you the best possible value return in your life.

Our lives needs to come with intention of being the champion of productivity, to have the mindset that you will accomplish things you have planned for the day, week, month, and year. Your productivity influences your action that leads you closer to your vision, goals, dreams, and aspiration. Unlocking your greatness definitely comes with productivity.

LET'S GET STARTED

It's a fact we cannot buy back time, so how do we effectively use our time better? In order to make successful changes, is to remove time wastage and replace it with productivity. Successful people are conscious of their time and want to ensure it is well spent and that it's cohesive, productive, concise, and outcome-driven.

In establishing the framework, we need to have the mindset to be ahead in a way that doesn't require overwhelm and procrastination.

Various tools you can use right now to de-clutter your mind:

Get two notebooks – One notebook should be for ideas. This will help you to write out any ideas that are on your mind. How many times have we experienced great ideas and all of a sudden we completely forget about it? The other notebook should be a goals notebook which will help you stay accountable of when you set and achieve your goals on a daily basis.

Smartphone – If you like accessibility and aren't keen on writing on paper, another way is to use your tablet or smartphone. When you turn it on to write something down, just be careful not to fall into the time-sucking trap of social media.

Productivity Discovery

There are six keys to assist you in identifying where you spend most of your time. These insights will help you get most of your time back and complete your tasks in the day feeling a sense of accomplishment and productivity.

Key 1 – Declutter

We are all filled with a lot of things in our mind that ranges from family, life, business, career, spouse/partner, current situations, and circumstances. It is those moments where we decide to be resourceful or not. If we choose not to be resourceful then the outcome will be overwhelm which leads to disorganization and loss of time in everything we do. So what is the next step? Use the declutter tools mentioned above and how you would input those goals into your daily week.

Key 2 – Elimination

It's time to get real and make a decision to remove certain things that are time wasters. For example, if TV time or social media robs your time, remove social media apps from your phone and cancel your TV subscriptions. Or remove items from your to do list that are not high value task and delegate to someone else, possibly hiring a virtual assistant. Don't think about eliminating your time wasters—do something about it.

Key 3 – Collation

Collate the amount of time spent on yourself that brings you value, whether it's your health, wealth, love, personal life, or happiness.

Key 4 – Systems & Priorities

There is a quote by Dale Beaumont: "Will I ever have to do this again? If it's a yes, build a system." When there isn't a system mechanism, you will burn out. Write out and systemize your approach. Identify repetitive areas that you know that can be streamlined and can be systemized, delegated, or outsourced.

Key 5 – Take out the 'No Time' belief

How many excuses have we said, "I don't have time," or "I don't have resources," or "I don't think I can do it?" This belief prevents you from everything you want to achieve in life.

Write out what you constantly say that is disempowering regarding time.

Write out a new belief that is empowering about time that is used wisely and effectively.

Key 6 – Application and Action

Now that these keys have been mentioned, don't waste another day by saying, "I will do it later." Take the challenge today so you have freed up time that matters most to you.

Today I have committed myself and completed the Productivity Discovery on Day_____ / Month_____ / Year_____

THE THREE-WAY CONFIDENCE TOOL FOR EFFECTIVENESS - THE SMART WAY OF PRODUCTIVITY

Have you heard of "Work smarter and not harder?" This is commonly used globally and universally. To be productive daily you need to create this habit:

- Make a decisive decision what is important
- Target one to two things you need to complete
- Be congruent with your values
- Focus to complete 100% of the time

Productivity is a learned skill which means you get better every single time you execute. Though you may feel at times you're not productive or have a few slip ups along the way, this is where your priorities and systemization come into place.

Unlocking your greatness through organization and prioritization comes from 3 phases.

Phase One – The Focused Zone

Great things only happen when you are out of your comfort zone. When you're focused, you will accomplish things at a faster rate.

Phase Two – The Action Zone

You learn by doing, and by doing you get smarter to finding what works in the process. Action is the key and it takes patience and resiliency. High achievers have a constant hunger attitude that never gives up in pursuing their dreams and goals that also should be modelled.

Phase Three – The Follow-Through Zone

The follow-through approach is crucial to your productivity this helps you engage effectively to prioritize and take control of your day. This will transform you into a driven person.

NINJA YOUR WAY THROUGH

Here are the NINJA Tools you can learn that will inspire you.

TOOL ONE – Ninja through your 'musts', not 'shoulds'

There are two perspectives when it comes to tasks you need to do. There are shoulds and musts. Shoulds is the easiest way to put in excuse and a must is where you can't place any excuses.

Applying the ninja way does not influence any deviation—its only mission is to completion. It works by starting from your mind right through to your action in the most efficient way possible where it's seamless.

The pitfalls in losing time and procrastinating leaves a lot of pressure to leaving things in the last minute. When you focus on small low value tasks that are not significant, it becomes a reoccurring pattern that influences you to be distracted such as web surfing, social media scrolling, etc., which is why you need to NINJA your must!

Choose your targets that are the most important tasks to do with the NINJA MOVE.

Select your most important "High Value" Tasks:

List Your Tasks	Prioritize and Select	Priority Order List
Item 1	Top 3 "High Value" Tasks	High Value 1
Item 2		High Value 2
Item 3		High Value 3
Item 4		Priority 1
Item 5		Priority 2
Item 6		Priority 3

Figure 3.0 High Value Tasks List

Apply the NINJA move and it will help you stay focused and prioritize your work load more effectively on the high valued tasks.

How to initiate your ninja move sequence:

- Go for one activity that must be done that day - No multi-tasking
- Identify your most Important task that is the highest value on your list
- Tackle your top 3 items after you have completed your important activity
- Take action immediately

TOOL TWO – The Eisenhower Matrix

This strategy comes from Dwight D Eisenhower, a president of the United States who served his country from 1953-1961, becoming the 34th lineage presidential chosen candidate.

One of the most-learned insights comes from his teaching regarding the Eisenhower matrix, popularly known as the urgent/important matrix. It is broken down into 4 quadrants.

As you can see in figure 4.0 - Top left is the urgent and important quadrant, the top right is not your urgent important quadrant. Bottom left is your unimportant and urgent, bottom right is not urgent and unimportant quadrant

	URGENT	NOT URGENT		URGENT	NOT URGENT
IMPORTANT	Q1	Q2	**IMPORTANT**	DO	PLAN
UNIMPORTANT	Q3	Q4	**UNIMPORTANT**	DELEGATE	ELIMINATE

Figure 4.0 Eisenhower Matrix

The matrix you see gives you the indication to categorize every task. This helps you to strategize your approach.

What is the difference? Urgent vs. Important.

Urgent: Items that require immediate attention and action.

Important: Items that are of great value which contributes to your values, mission and goals.

Q1 Must Do Now - This is where you invest your time, energy and attention. When the task is at Q1, strategically find better ways in the process to completing the tasks while you are in action.

Example: Deadlines, meetings, projects, milestones.

Q2 Schedule & Focus - Planning time for personal development. This is where you schedule important things intentionally while they're not urgent.

Example: Finding better ways in life, creating systems that streamline what you do, personal growth, and relaxation.

Q3 Delegate or Avoid - These tasks are urgent however it consumes your time to not be productive. This is where items can be delegated.

Example: Some phone calls, some emails and out of scope meetings, etc. Interruptions and distractions.

Q4 Stop & Avoid - This is the procrastination and waste of time quadrant. These are the tasks that do not provide any value at all.

Example: Social media surfing, TV surfing, games, various breaks, coffee breaks, etc.

Don't spend any time here at all, unless:

- Your work is social media
- Your break comes from a productive meeting and tasks are being completed.

To achieve the highest outputs there are two simple steps:
Step 1 - Focus on Q1 & Q2 by eliminating Q4 to resolve Q3 activities.
Step 2 - After you have completed your Q1, invest most of your time in Q2.

TOOL THREE – Pareto Principle or 80/20 Rule

The Pareto Principle, the 80/20 rule was created by the Italian economist and sociologist, Vilfredo Pareto, who observed that 80% of effects stem from only 20% of causes.

This principle has been acknowledged by other industry experts and used in all different forms. This rule identifies and evaluates decisions, processes and patterns in getting a specific results.

An example would be 80% of profits are generated by the 20% of products. So how does it apply in our lives? 20% of your highest value tasks brings in the 80% of significant results. When you prioritize and schedule effectively the outcome of your results will be evident. The purpose of using the Pareto Principle is to maximize your time, effort, energy, resources, and money.

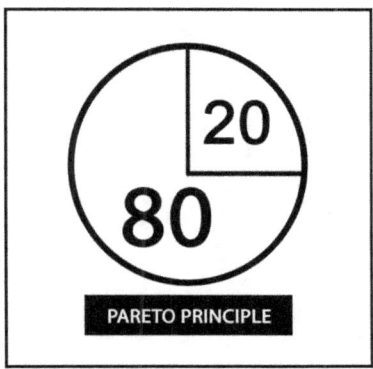

Figure 5.0 Pareto Principle

Putting this into practice, when putting your tasks together and identifying your most important activities the questions you need to answer is: Which of the high value 20% tasks would give you the most impact?

What are the 20% most important tasks that give you best use of time, energy, and money?

Utilizing the three tools would enhance your productivity and take your greatness to the next level. This will help your approach effectively.

ACTION STEPS

Developing your own personal system will bring you to success and setting up the process and executing will pay huge dividends in your life.

- When you get stuck, what type of excuses are you running in your mind?
- What must you do to set yourself for success when it comes to prioritization?
- Write out your top 3 strategies you need to be productive you know you can achieve.
- What are the tools you can use that can help you stay on track and accountable?
- If you could do one thing different what would it be when it comes to productivity?

CHAPTER 7

PROTECT THE CULTURE VIBE

"Surround yourself with people who are only going to lift you higher"
– Oprah Winfrey

MODEL OF EXCELLENCE AND STANDARDS

It's a fact that we all want to succeed in life and the people around us can either build us or sway us from our destiny in life. So in this chapter we will be covering the aspects of surroundings, environment, and accountability including the power of mentoring and mastermind groups. It's these elements of an empowered culture that shapes you to success that unleashes your greatness at a rapid rate.

When you are surrounded by vision builders, influencers, action takers, purpose-driven leaders, contributors of value, and successful people in their line of expertise, you will learn how they think, respond, and take action.

Synergizing and re-wiring your mindset by networking in this arena can catapult you to the next level. You will start to understand how others face their challenges and overcome with confidence and resolve.

It's those moments you want to really engage and focus that you wouldn't want to re-invent the wheel and do things on your own—that takes forever.

You would rather be a student to learn from someone who has success and fast track your progress.

CIRCLE OF INFLUENCE

Jim Rohn quotes: "You are the average of the five people you spend the most time with."

When you are faced with the decision of who you want to spend your time with, it can be a challenge when your friends have different mindsets than you do. However, if you want to succeed in life, then we need to look at who your circle of friends are through a different lens.

The question you need to ask yourself is: are they positively impacting your life? Do they believe in you and encourage you to go out their way to help you? Do they tell you the truth? Or are they just time fillers, wasting time to doing nothing that brings fulfilment? Or are they completely opposite and don't add value? Your personal progress depends on your circle of influence. If you compromise and know it doesn't serve your passion and purpose, eventually sooner or later you will become the same as them. Whatever their traits, habits, lingo, and lifestyle, you will be influenced in the same manner. The truth is that your inner circle has a major influence toward standards.

When you purposely surround yourself with successful people, you will naturally set high standards of excellence to constantly improve your life for the better. This is what greatness is all about: tapping into resources to learn, grow, expand, and evolve.

So here is where the rubber meets the road. If you truly want to take your life to the next level and achieve real results that open the door for an epic life, rather than procrastinating, it's time you draw the line and set high standards. Remember you live life by your design.

I did my personal strategy to draw the line when it came to my circle of friends and it was difficult. I had to do something about it or else I would remain the same. The aim was not to alienate my friends and be a total jerk, it was to be smart in how I utilize my time. I can still have friends, I just need to place my limits and choose my investment of time. Your time is valuable because you can never get it back. However, what you do can make an impact to your future or not. Is your time being spent bringing value to yourself and others? Does it support collaboration and positive impact for growth and contribution towards your life? Are you encouraged to think with perspective and meaning that brings fulfilment and happiness? If not, then you need to reevaluate your life.

Take the courage to make a game plan and iron it out. Are you up for the 5 Step Friends Challenge?

Step 1 - Get a piece of paper

Step 2 - Draw a line in the middle

Step 3 - Left hand side note down on the title (Positive Friends) and Right hand note down on the title (Negative Friends)

Step 4 - Go to your smartphone and list out your friends out

Step 5 - List your Top 5 who would be your Positive Friends. List out your Top 5 who would be your Negative Friends.

UNDERSTANDING YOUR ENVIRONMENT THAT SUPPORTS YOUR GROWTH

Now that you have tackled that challenging task, the next action is to understand your environment and where you're situated. There are four P's towards greatness that gives you the gauge to always look for when you want to ensure your positive environment continues to give you momentum and push in life. Four insights that will show you how you can strengthen your environment that rewires your mind to think through circumstances, situation and people around you. Does your current environment you are living right now inspire you to give back? The four P's listed gives you simple practicalities of your environment and others.

Potential

We all have the potential to expand and be the best version of ourselves. When you see that there's potential and opportunities around you, you must take necessary steps to unlock your potential to greater capacity.

Purpose

Knowing and living your purpose have different distinctions. We can acknowledge our purpose, but without being deliberate in experiencing it, it can cause setbacks of passion, enthusiasm, and focus. When you realize your purpose and you serve your purpose, this definitely helps you get a different perspective.

Performance

Success comes to those who take action that does not allow procrastination. Realizing your potential and activating your purpose stirs you take action and become outcome driven. You will start to create empowering habits to always make things happen that means you plan, execute and improve.

Personal Growth

We should never think we've learned everything and stop learning. Learning is a process and there are always new things to grasp. When you constantly invest in yourself through personal development, you become a significant, high-valued asset.

POWER OF ENVIRONMENT

Most people probably know who Michael Jordan is. He is one of the greatest basketball players who ever lived. Till this day there are aspiring basketball players who want to be like MJ. Even some of them playing the sport in the NBA strive to match and surpass his greatness.

Air Jordan is a staple name and his influence towards the sports, ownership of an NBA club, endorsements, and signature shoes is significant. I can say this that Michael Jordan build his game, created habits, and developed his own unmatched work ethics from the ground up. Constantly improving his game, learning valuable lessons from mistakes, failures, and taking it to the next level made him a formidable, unstoppable player in the NBA.

This is what he had to say, "I've missed more than 9000 shots in my career. I've lost almost 300 games. Twenty-six times I've been trusted to take the game winning shot and missed. I've failed over and over and over again in my life and that is why I succeed."

If you change your perspective about what failure is, you will succeed.

Every time you fail and make a mistake is another step forward upwards to where you want to go in life. If you focus on the details, you will change the landscape of your success. Michael Jordan has won 6 NBA Championships, however, his quest to winning was sheer effort of team work. The entire Chicago Bulls squad worked together to win.

One superstar cannot do this alone.

Growing up I played basketball religiously. I love the sport and started competing at seven years of age up to my teens. During that period I experienced winning championships, played at a state level, travelled interstate in Australia, and it was wonderful. Just like any game when you know that you need to be at your best, it all begins from training and the amount of hours you put in. You work very hard in drills, and have endless practice on court to get your shot up through the hoop. The key to winning and having momentum in basketball is teamwork and heart.

One of the greatest coaches in NBA Basketball is Phil Jackson. He perfectly stated this quote: "The strength of the team is each individual member. The strength of each member is the team." This is the very reason why he has won eleven championship rings in total as a coach, the most in history both for the Chicago Bulls and Los Angeles Lakers.

As talented you may be in life, the surroundings and influences are the most importance. You can be as positive as want you to be, be more passionate, energetic, and enthusiastic about many things but as soon you are in a crowd who's completely opposite, it can potentially derail you and do a lot of harm in the way you think or do.

Looking back on my life I use to get annoyed with my parents, always hammering me about the people I hang with and parents tend to see things differently. I can speak with honesty that parents have perspective because I'm a parent myself. When you're surrounded with people that don't have the same values as you, that compromises your faith in what you do and who you are as person. This can influence and lead you in a different direction that is not empowering and inspiring.

I know this first hand. When I was with a different crowd, that life is all about the parties. Temporally it was fun in the moment, however, it starts to wear off and wasn't fulfilling my future at all.

I believe it's our responsibility to choose who we associate with. To this day it has stuck by me in my mind that: "The closest people you're with and the books you read is the type of person you will become." There's a lot of truth in this. I knew from within that in order for me to live an epic life and be a success, I need to take ownership over my life to choose my environment and people that I network and connect with. If you don't, it will lead you down a path that you don't want for your life.

To be in a winning team, you have to be associated with like-minded people who are determined, focused, result-oriented, and purpose-driven who are positively impacting. In reality it will rewire you to be that way.

BE BOLD, BE BRAVE AND COMMIT

If you're in a positive environment it makes you bold, brave, and committed to your vision and mission. I remember there was an advertisement banner promoting a certain university on a side panel of a commercial bus. It stated,

> **fierce, determined and ready to take action**

"Be Bold, Be Brave, & Commit." I saw this whilst waiting at a red light heading to the gym. I noticed not only the words on the bus but a person's face who looked *fierce, determined* and *ready to take action*. We all know that action speaks louder than words and everyone who comes across this advertisement will have a different perspective about this particular promo.

As soon as I entered the gym and during my workout, all I was pondering was those three empowering statements: "Be Brave! Be Bold! Commit!" It got me thinking and fired up.

Though the ad was for potential university students, it gave me perspective. I see this marketing message that their brand is all about culture and to those who join the university will be transformed into the future they want for their lives. If the purposes and values of the university is about transformation into taking action, then its environment of people would have the same goals and aspiration towards education. Students will learn, grow, graduate, and tackle the world with courage, boldness, and direction.

So in reflection, the environment you are in will shape you. It's important to have awareness to know the values, purpose, mission, vision, and culture of the people you associate with and the group of environment that you spend most of your time with.

SEEK OUT MENTORS

According to Wikipedia, mentorship is a relationship in which a more experienced or more knowledgeable person helps guides a less experienced or less knowledgeable person.

Having mentors and investing in a mentor is important for growth and success. Though I'm a coach and speaker, I too have mentors for every aspect of my life. I may know certain things, but I don't know all things.

Mentors can be a person you know who will add value to your life, who doesn't beat around the bush, and tells you the truth even if it hurts. Sometimes I have coffee chats with my mentors and learn how they process things with their mindset right through to action. I see mentors who have gone before me who have tons of experience that I can learn from and that is a huge bonus to have. In other words, I can avoid their setbacks completely and apply the smarts towards my personal journey.

So make a list of each area you want to be mentored in whether it be in finance, relationship, health, marriage, etc. This is not a get a quick mentor type of thing. It does take time for relationships to be developed when you find a mentor. Other forms of mentors can also be in a form of a book. Their knowledge and experience is written and you still can learn and grow.

MASTERMIND GROUPS & ACCOUNTABILITY

If you truly want to experience complete acceleration for success then a mastermind group and accountability is the ultimate key.

There are choices and decisions that need to be made and it's a pivotal turning point. We either choose a ferry boat that takes longer or an advanced speed boat. The choice is ours and sometimes our ego and pride is the stumbling block. Understanding our strengths and challenges and letting go of our ego will help us connect with people who are positively driven and uplifting.

Every successful person has formed their own mastermind groups and accountability partners such as Andrew Carnegie, Henry Ford, and many others in today's generation.

Mastermind groups are like the Super Heroes of Marvel Avengers. I remember a movie scene where they were teaming up together for the first time such as Thor, Hulk, Captain America, Iron Man, Black Widow, Hawkeye, and Nick Fury, just to name a few. They were discussing together their action plan toward the enemy.

Mastermind groups is where members focus and share their efforts, energy, and time together. It is simply made of a tightly-knit group between five to eight people where meetings are conducted either face to face or on conference calls online that are organized between weekly, fortnightly or monthly. This is where knowledge, experience, stories, and resources are shared amongst members which can provide a significant positive impact towards learning and inspiration.

Members who are specialists in their respective field help each other and come together for a cause to tackle challenges, work through business issues, or gain insights towards any personal life agendas. These type of dynamics can flow into problem solving, brainstorming, motivation, and improvements towards life and business—and most importantly, get honest feedback.

GET EMPOWERED BY ACCOUNTABILITY

Power of accountability is the follow-through feedback that keeps you in check of your progress by doing what you say and saying what you do. The issues that a lot of people face when it comes to taking action and thinking forward with their goals and vision is the lack of two common areas: commitment and accountability. Mastermind groups are a great strategy to have for creating accountability.

When you apply the accountability factor, these are the questions that need to be filtered for greater impact:

1. Have you accomplished to what you have set out to do?
2. What were the challenges you faced?
3. What will be your next step and focus?

It's these simple questions that aligns your accountability benchmarks.

How do mastermind groups work?

You may be asking right now, how do I start one? Find people who fit your purpose and values, seek out those who are like-minded and committed. If your goal is to be successful and to become a millionaire then it's people with the same goals you need to ask. You will never know till you ask. High-caliber people would like to be in an empowered group that are focused and committed.

Don't wait for a mastermind group to form on its own because it will never happen. Go out there and make it happen. The sooner the better and the faster you will accelerate with the high-performing people you want to associate with.

DON'T FORGET TO NETWORK

I remember a time when my mentor gave me real constructive feedback. He asked me how my business was doing and I said it was okay. Then he asked how many people I was seeing and networking per week. I said at least two people every fortnight.

I knew then that wasn't the benchmark I was going for. If I wanted my business to grow and meet like-minded people who are also striving for greatness and are successful in their fields, I needed to make an effort every week to go to networking events.

This is how conversations flow and connecting with others will help me with accountability and mastermind groups. Connections don't just appear out of thin air. It requires you to go out there and connect, engage, and network. Networking is important, so find the right group of people that have the same values, purpose, and focus that will enrich your life as well as others.

In this chapter we have covered circles of friends and peers who are like-minded and purpose driven, and those who are not. The insights and steps outlined helps you progress further towards greatness including the motivation to thrive forward with excellence. When your environment is covered and empowered for progress, you will make a significant impact in your personal life and the people around you.

ACTION STEPS

It's all about culture, connection, and collaboration. When you surround yourself with the right kind of people who empower you, you become unstoppable in your purpose.

- As you have just learned about circle of friends, go through the 5 Steps Friends Challenge.
- How important is it to be surrounded with like-minded people in your life?
- What do you need to do now that will help your circle of influence to be more positive and impacting?
- How have these insights towards masterminds and accountability helped you with your future and why?

Who is your accountability buddy? If you don't have one yet, list out who can be your buddy and will keep you accountable towards your journey and where you want to go in life.

CHAPTER 8

EYE OF THE TIGER

"Patience, persistence and perspiration makes an unbeatable combination for success."
– Napoleon Hill

Have you ever met or know someone who is persistent? They always strive in focusing on what they want. These are the type of people who are go getters and won't take no for an answer. They can be perceived as annoying and over the top. It's normally what the general public think.

On the other side of the spectrum, a person who is persistent are those who are purpose-driven with their goals and dreams in what they want to achieve. Over time, persistent people build a thick skin of not getting personal with situations and enjoy the fulfilment of accomplishing something. In other words, they take action, and they understand that time is the essence of everything.

The perspective of persistence is to train your internal muscles to not give up, to improve in developing personal development that transforms into tenacity and grit.

So a formula for the work ethics behind the persistency that empowers your motivation for greatness are these five actions:

1. Unpack your personal persistence factor.
2. Develop and take your winning attitude to the highest levels for success.

3. Turn your confidence into results.
4. Learn how to take feedback and build internal muscles through adversity.
5. Develop your inner patience and still experience personal breakthroughs.

It's these elements in this chapter that will pave the way to greatness.

BE PERSISTENT EVERY TIME

Basically it means to never stop moving.

The definition of persistence on dictionary.com is *'the quality of being persistent.'* Basically it means to never stop moving. If we take persistence to the thesaurus, it's translated as *endurance, perseverance, tenacity, grit and resolution.*

Persistence is not about being an annoying pest that is lurking around in front of your face. Persistence is all about focus, consistency, impact and grit!

What I've noticed that the more you are focus on what you do best, you become resilient and vision-focused. We live in a world with all sorts of distractions that kills our opportunity of being productive and effective. Have you heard of Netflix? Have you heard of 'Insta' (Instagram)? Have you heard of Facebook? Nothing wrong with these cool platforms, but you can get stuck in a vortex for a long time by non-stop scrolling, liking, posting and sharing. It becomes an addiction. If used incorrectly this can eat up your time to what matters most and that is results.

Persistence can mean a lot of different things and how I see for purpose on this chapter is all about achieving your goals, accomplishing your milestones, and honing your passion.

So how do we develop persistence? There are four ways.

Key 1 – Live your life on purpose

"Never consider the possibility of failure, as long as you persist, you will be successful." -Brian Tracy

I think we have heard the word of purpose a million times from various media, blogs, videos, articles, and speakers, but I believe it's relevant in today's generation that we all need to have purpose and direction. Without the clarity you cannot progress. The power of purpose is the key to your development of persistence, it's your driving force that empowers your **REASONS & WHYS**.

I heard a powerful podcast from Les Brown, motivational speaker. He said how to empower your motivation without losing it is to write out 5 reasons as to why you deserve it. This means if you continue to work hard and smart towards your greatness, then list the reasons why you deserve an epic life. So if you are persisting on reaching your goals and dreams, then live a purpose-driven life that inspires you to achieve it.

Key 2 – Be specific with your planning

"Plans are nothing, planning is everything." -Dwight D Eisenhower

To be persistent is being intentional with your approach with focus and grit. This influences how you plan effectively in detail which many people tend to not be bothered in paying attention to the specifics. I realize that many successful people in their field of expertise go into the granular details. For example, if it's in business, you would know the ins and outs of the operations, logistics and forecasting numbers of profit and losses. If its health, you don't just eat healthy food. It's about being specific to what you eat, how many calories consumed, what type of food that affects your results. If it's personal development, discovering and taking action to where your gaps and challenges are and constantly working it through to be your strengths. Planning comes with strategic action which is crucial to your success and here is how you can implement your planning strategy.

Figure 6.0 Planning Strategy

As you can see on figure 6.0 when you go through the planning stage there are questions you need to ask yourself so you can ensure that action is taken place.

(*Planning* starts with your goals) Questions – Where do you want to go? Where is your destination? Does this road lead you to fulfilment?

(*Planning* opens your perspective of your desired outcomes) Questions – How do I get there? What are the specific areas that will get me closer? What type of strategy is needed to achieve my outcomes?

(Planning gives you to focus on your targets) Questions – What are the measurements to hitting your targets? What type of results would you need to get it? What would be the KPI's would you have set that keeps you on track?

(Planning encourages you to improve and expand) Questions – What can I do to improve? What will it give me to know the areas of improvement?

When you have a plan and it is well prepared, you bring boosting confidence to your persistence. So right now write out your plan in what you want and add in your smarts to it.

Key 3 – Strengthen your mindset

Mindset is everything and having growth mindset trumps fix mindset.

Check out the difference between the both mindsets and apply how you can strengthen your mindset for success when it comes to persistence.

Fixed Mindset	Growth Mindset
Avoids challenges	Thrives on challenges
Offended by feedback	Learns from feedback
Doesn't feel the need to improve	Seeks constant feedback
No effort and energy	Brings effort and energy
Gives up and loses hope	Does not give up or give in
Failure mentality and negative self-belief	Affirming and breaks through setbacks
Threatened by others success	Inspired by others success
Thinks about self	Provides constant value
Victim mentality	Victor mentality
Blames, justifies and no responsibility	Takes ownership and responsibility

Key 4 – Choosing your association is a must

It is our responsibility to choose our association. Either it will be positive or negative. There are two ways that can happen. When you don't take action or ownership of your surroundings, you will end up with the wrong crowd. They may be your friends, but they may not empower you or believe in your purpose.

On the other end, when you choose to be with the right positive people, you will start surrounding yourself in an environment that is impacting, encouraging, and definitely inspiring to add more value into your life.

Developing your persistence and applying these keys can you help you stay focused on what matters most and the goals you want to achieve in life. We all know down the track that there will be challenges, but when you apply the keys mentioned, this will take your persistence to the next level. This is when persistence turns into momentum. When you are on a mission you become unstoppable with your pursuit.

DEVELOP YOUR WINNING ATTITUDE

When persistence is applied, the winning attitude becomes more evident. We all have seen and experience different types of attitudes and they are the good, the bad, the negative, the positive, the defeated and the winning. Most people tend to think that attitude is predominantly behavior, however, it's also the thinking preferences (our mindset) that influences our emotions through our actions. This means we choose our attitude, and how we tackle situations and circumstances in our day. Whether we take up a great attitude or not, the ball is always in your court. You are the captain of your ship and you hold the power towards your attitude.

BUILD YOUR HOUSE THAT IS A FIRM FOUNDATION

I remember a time when my son had different phases of watching certain cartoon movies and shows. It started with the Wiggles, Sesame Street, Lion King, Toy Story (1, 2, and 3) and the list goes on. If you have kids you know exactly what I mean. If you know any kids, they seem to have new different flavors every single time, which only lasts them for a short while till they see a new bright and shiny new thing. There was a particular clip on YouTube kids my son played. He was only three years old at the time. I can't believe kids nowadays how they can wiz their way into scrolling through different apps. The clip that he was watching was the three little pigs and big bad wolf. So my son wanted to copy the short clip and build his own house using Jenga blocks and pretended to be the big bad wolf to blow it down. With great success, the blocks fell down and he felt powerful and happy at the same time.

So he then built another house using the plastic connector blocks. I was laughing inside because it was funny to see the entire process. He got so upset that he couldn't blow it off as the blocks were interconnected and out of frustration he threw a huge baby tantrum. As I witnessed this before my eyes it really got me thinking and an aha moment popped in my head.

I was so taken by this insight about houses being built the right way. My take on this experience is that when you build your life upon a solid foundation that's firm, no winds or storms can ever move you. The analogy of the foundation I'm referring to is your why, reasons, values, purpose, vision and mission. These so called storms are your negativity, setbacks or situations which will eventually pass by. If you look at nature itself the storms are not permanent, so be encouraged today that storms it will not be there forever.

To avoid the personal dramas, take special note to not be like the others where the storm has passed by and yet in their mindset they still carry the storm. Know this and engrave into your heart that you are stronger than you think. It's required to weather the storm and stand firm. Have absolute optimism with a winning attitude to rise and conquer. Don't give up on your goals, don't throw your dreams away, and never tell yourself you can't. Everything inside you is greatness. All you need to do is unleash the empowering super hero from within.

The purpose of a winning attitude is despite the chaos, challenges and adversity, the mindset and perspective is that you are unstoppable, uncontainable and unbreakable. Nothing in life is easy, however, the winning attitude is the game changer in looking at things in a different lens of resourcefulness.

So how do we live an empowered life that develops a winning attitude?

Be the person who is a champion, who is a winner in life. Never let doubt creep in that will hold you down. You don't need to fake it to make it. Be that person who is real who makes it. Winning Attitude is a strategy that builds the inner lion of strength and an eagle of precise vision.

THREE STEP APPROACH TOWARDS A WINNING ATTITUDE

Step 1 – Create a winner's mind frame

Make the choice and decision to be self-disciplined. Winners don't quit, they religiously work on themselves and protect their mind. Setup your network that supports your growth and empowers you to be great.

Step 2 – Build stepping stones of your ascension

Be so result-driven that you become accountable for progress. Setup key measures and benchmarks to constantly evolve. Be the person of contribution and hope that brings value that's bigger than yourself.

Step 3 – Can-do attitude

Play at a higher level when it comes to your high value activities. Commit, focus, and constantly improve your life with a can-do attitude.

Your hunger drive for greatness is what will set you for success. It's this emotional factor that connects all the dots. Insatiable hunger for success unlocks the winning attitude.

CONFIDENCE IS YOUR WAY OF SAYING THAT YOU CAN DO IT

In this day and age, confidence is an important factor when it comes to be an industry changer, action taker, visionary builder, and high achiever. Even when often times your confidence is not there with all the jitters and nerves.
What if there was a solution to turn those jitters around to becoming a confident person that constantly builds the inner muscle of an empowered self-esteem? Wouldn't that be life changing? I believe everyone has that potential.

Confidence is a habit.

There are seven practical tips to boosting and increasing your self-confidence. When it comes to successful habits, confidence is inbuilt by acknowledging common factors that potentially hold us back in shifting the mindset. There are many factors that can hinder our confidence like fear, worry, doubts and uncertainty. I know from experience and the book by Susan Jeffers *Feel the Fear and Do It Anyway* has been an eye opener. It really doesn't matter if your fearful, just get on with it and do it. We play so many stories inside our mind and never seem to progress in life. Confidence is the opposite. It doesn't matter if you suck at it, the more confident you are, the self-belief is empowered and it's the key to success. Knowing who you are with the beauty of understanding your self-worth takes confidence out of this world.

BE CONFIDENT AND SHOW IT

How do we become confident when we don't feel it?

You have to build your confidence muscle, just like building your thick skin. You just have to roll with the punches and keep on moving till it becomes second nature.

Till this day, I remember when I was invited to be a guest speaker for a church youth night. I freaked out because I was a total newbie, not knowing anything.

I questioned myself, how could God do this to me? I felt a huge fear and I still went for it, I said yes to giving it a try. Looking back now, I thank God I went through that ordeal and pain. Working through the process in a sermon was challenging, though I gave it my best by writing eight pages' worth and spoke directly to my notes instead of facing the congregation. The whole time my head was placed downwards, so no one could see my face of sweat and nervousness.

Now tell me, isn't that embarrassing? Over time I practiced and practiced and continued to work on developing my craft on speaking. Was I nervous? Yes. Do I still get nervous? Only for a couple of seconds till I own the moment.

In my late twenties I was actually surprised that I found out from my mother that when I was a small child I had speech problems. She was so worried about me she took me to speech therapist. As a religious mother she prayed, believed, and had faith that I will be ok.

After months of therapy my speech developed and I was able to speak. Fast track today, I'm a motivational speaker! Sounds crazy, right? Where ever you are right now in life your past cannot dictate your future. You can stir your destiny by the decision you make today. If you want to live an epic life that inspires your greatness to greater heights then I say, go for it! You have only one life to live, so live it!

Confidence in yourself plays a huge part to living an epic life. If you don't love yourself, then your self-belief will be affected. The flipside to making confidence work for you is applying every step of the chapters in this book.

There are couple of insider tips from experience I do that removes any jitters when nerves starts to kick-in, especially when I do public speaking. I want to spread my influence and confidence by being courageous and fearless. There are 7 practical strategies to boost your self-esteem that influence your self-confidence.

STARTING POINT FOR CONFIDENCE IS AFFIRMATION AND ACTIONS

Confidence is very simple and many people make it complicated to the point that they are stuck. Your positive vision and how you see things in perspective including the affirmations you tell yourself is what you will create. It doesn't appear on your lap. It's up to you to take that responsibility and make it work. Your self-esteem becomes more evident when your beliefs about yourself are empowering. When you are grateful, thankful, and have a positive outlook in how you see things in different perspectives it changes limitations into limitless possibilities. Your mindset is shifted and your physiology towards these challenges turns into courage.

Practical Tip 1 – Confidence is about being the part, looking the part and fitting the part

T. Harver says that your inner world creates your outer world, which means the outer you is the reflection of your inner you.

Your confidence levels may not be there yet and that's ok. Be an actor to play the part of a confident person because you will morph into one. Just remember every successful person all started from the beginning and worked to the top. No one is immune to this, so take the courage to work from the ground up.

Practical Tip 2 – The makeover

There is nothing wrong in working through your self-esteem and image. I'm a fan when it comes to makeovers, to see how a person was before and after, particularly body transformation because you get to see the end-results. It's definitely the same principles when you work on yourself for transformation and everything about you changes for confidence.

Practical Tip 3 – Your thoughts and what you say about yourself

Thoughts and statements you say to yourself have a major impact. So stay in the positive lane and only say and think positive thoughts that inspires and empowers you.

Practical Tip 4 – Know thyself

When you are self-aware of your life, it gives you a competitive advantage to do something about it. Always come with intention to Karate chop any negativity which is easy to do. Instead continuing to self-affirm yourself that you can, that you will and you must.

Practical Tip 5 – Reading inspiring biographies and stories

Associating yourself with inspiring stories encourages yourself to be inspiring. Reading and applying life principles can make a significant impact in your life. Biographies that show that how others did it are inspiring.

Practical Tip 6 – Give value to others

Being kind and generous is about value to others. You know the feeling when your self-esteem is low and it feels wonderful when someone injects inspiration, hope and life in your self-belief.

Have an environment around that supports you and continue to give value to others.

Practical Tip 7 Challenge yourself past the limits

Never be satisfied where you are. Every successful person who ever lived on this earth challenge themselves to achieving excellence. It's a standard that they will not stop till they reach it. A perfect example is Thomas Edison who experienced unsuccessful attempts and failed 1000 at inventing the light bulb. Then one successful experiment changed his life and the lives of many others. Or how Steve Jobs with Apple has revolutionized in the way we interact with smartphones.

DO SOMETHING WHEN YOU GET STUCK

Sometimes in life it's not a bed of roses. We live on this earth and it's bound for challenges, issues, problems, unwanted circumstances, and the list goes on. These types of situations can get us stuck, stagnant, and nowhere to move. Have you experienced this a lot? Don't be afraid or scared if you are stuck in a rut. Get yourself up and become resourceful and think from a different perspective. Here's a quick tip I do that gets me out of being stuck.

- Own up and take responsibility to rise and conquer.
- Remind yourself of your purpose, values, mission and vision. See your progress and destination and not past regrets.
- Refocus and get activated again.

PATIENCE & PERSEVERANCE

When you are striving and aiming for something, always have two important attributes: patience and perseverance. I know from experience and the experience of others that there isn't any microwave instant success. It takes time in the right way, however, it doesn't mean you need to slow down your progress. We are all on a different journey and never compare yourself with others. Only compete with yourself to getting better and you will see results.

Every time I see a social media post, comment, or a blog article about patience, it reminds me that you need to work on your craft and be smart by being resilient, persistent, and focus behind the scenes. Then your success will make the loudest noise.

ACTION STEPS

Having the right attitude is everything. It teaches you resiliency, focus, and determination. Never lose your positive outlook attitude.

- What would be your strengths and weaknesses when it comes to planning?
- What are your insights that you've learned on persistency?
- Why is having an empowering and winning attitude important?
- Identify the areas you need confidence in, and what you need to do to improve.
- How would you elevate your self-esteem that enhances your self-confidence?

PART 3:
GREATNESS IS GRATITUDE AND PERSPECTIVE

CHAPTER 9

RISE IN YOUR INNER

"With the new day comes new strength and new thoughts."
– Eleanor Roosevelt

IMPORTANCE OF BOTH

In this chapter you will discover how to rise in your inner that identifies your internal being that coincides with love, happiness, wealth, and your health. The approach taken is to internalize from within that influences your greatness to the outer which is your external being that is the reflection of your life. What this means is everything to this point from each chapter helps you to unlock and unleash your inner motivation for success.

Here's how it all fits.

- Our internal life influences our external which is mindset to actions.
- Our external influences our internal life which is actions to mindset.

Both aspects play an important part one way or the other. We need to understand that our inner, which is our mindset, translates into the outer which is our actions. The purpose as to why we need to learn both our inner and outer perspectives is to show the bigger picture in how you see your life.

There are many perspectives around this concept and the aim is to provide a foundational framework that is simple and easy to grasp with no gimmicks.

How we rise from our inner and tap into success are the insights that feed into the four pillars that empower you to live an epic life. Before we dig deeper, here are the four pillars of life. Figure 6.0 shows each pillar of the infrastructure with no particular order.

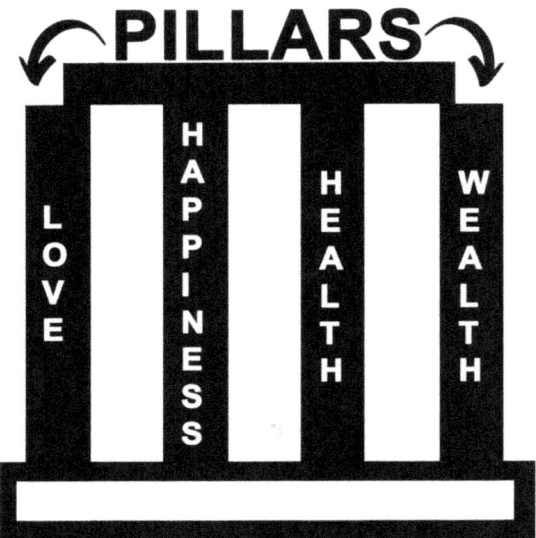

Figure 6.0 Pillars of life

The formula of the Pillars

Love + Happiness = Inner

Health + Wealth = Outer

It's important to understand that without the emotions of your inner why and what makes you happy, including the relationships you build, can either encourage you to live life at its fullest or discourage you to be the victim and not enjoy life at all.

We need to realize that we are the captain of our ship and the master of our destiny. This means we have the power of choice to make things happen or give up in attempting to do anything that gives you fulfilment.

First of all, let's talk about hacks. What is a hack? Most people have different ideas to what a hack is. A hack is basically a short cut or easier way of doing something. Generally speaking, people tend to think that hack is someone hacking into your computer. If we were to simplify it in an informal way that is positive, then a hack is executing and finding more effective ways to do something. It is cutting through the B.S (Baloney Sandwich) of excuses, and taking action that is smart, effective, and produces high value in return.

So what is an inner success hack? It focuses on unleashing your inner hunger for success, having fulfilling relationships around you that is living in the simple art of happiness. Applying the principles mentioned in this book and combining the inner hacks can significantly boost your self-esteem and confidence, in which you will start to notice the internal changes. The transformation that occurs from within will change the external ways of your life as, your inner world creates and influences your outer world.

People say that money can't buy you happiness, though it can give you an experience and options. If we were to give a few examples, a person may be very wealthy, however, he is deeply depressed, anxious, and worried about life. Or a person could be healthy, but may have marital and relationship problems. I know this can be extreme scenarios, but to dig deeper, it's important to know how your state of mind is and where you are internally focused towards fulfilment, meaning, and happiness. Being internally happy is one of the main game changers that supersedes motivation without the hype because your outlook in life becomes more positive and genuine.

The focus to being internally successful is your inner being. It is your mindset, it's how you respond and see things in perspective. So what are the steps to this? Firstly, empowering your relationships around you and secondly being at the state of happiness.

These pillars mentioned are your guide and reference to give you that self-awareness and an opportunity to take action to live life. Every pillar is a gauge in where you know you can improve and tackle what's important to you.

LOVE AND RELATIONSHIPS

Motivation is void when you are not creating and building meaningful relationships around you. It's the source of energy of encouragement and support that propels you to the next level.

I believe meaningful relationships are important, as they create memories, experiences, and moments. Love is a powerful emotion and its one of my values for connection because it's where you experience joy.

We all want to have connection, to love and be loved, and to be part of a family, tribe, or group. We experience fulfilment of joy through connection of human interaction relationships. Our fears are also the same. The fear of not belonging, not being loved, and not being enough. Gratitude plays a significant part through relationships. Unlocking your greatness is not about the book on love you may find in the book store, it's about taking your experience of relationships and love to the next level with effort and meaning.

Everything in life revolves around relationships. There are key insights in building meaningful relationships that are universal and fundamental for love, life, and business.

Our internal relationships influence our external relationships.

There have been a lot of books on personal development, particularly on a principle that says your outer world is created by your inner world.

So our experience in life on the outside reflects or conveys the internal relationship of ourselves. What this means if you're hating life and have self-taught stories that everyone takes advantage of you or you don't deserve the best things in life, it becomes your life story.

If you reverse engineer your mindset from these stories, then there needs to be a shift of thinking. Think thoughts of abundance, that you're taking opportunities, and you're experiencing fulfilment every day. Having this type of perspective, how will your relationship look like if you stepped outside the box? Seeing it from a different lens? It will certainly feel a lot different.

Meaningful relationships is the outcome of how we build successful relationships internally.

Whether it's in business, life or relationships, the success is built inwardly.

10 INSIGHTS OF MEANINGFUL RELATIONSHIPS

1. Let your mindset be on giving end.

When your focus and values are to give unconditionally it creates connection. Have you ever experienced in life when meeting someone you felt instant connection like you've known each other for a long time? I know that I have. The science behind this is when you focus on giving, it reflects in your posture, tonality of your voice, and in your movements.

2. Behavioral flexibility towards serving

We must have an understanding that everyone is different in terms of relationships. Every individual has different versions and perspectives on what relationships mean to them. So to have behavioral flexibility and adaptability is to serve others in how you would want to be served. So how do we improve meaningful relationships? Commit with an approach to seek in understanding first, then to be understood, and that's how you serve others effectively.

3. Relationships is all about giving and receiving

Have you heard of the word it takes two to tango? Or meeting half way? In a relationship it takes both ends to make it work and that means to give and to receive. Most people find it a huge challenge to either receive or to even give. We should always be the person to have an opportunity for both.

4. We are all different

The most wonderful thing in mankind is that we are uniquely different in the ways of life, thoughts, values and purpose.

    The key to great relationships is empathy with understanding. Each person has their own world of thinking, their own map and how they experience it every day. To build effective relationships is to have the awareness of empathy knowing to tap in their map how they see, feel and think of their own world. It is a key strategy to connect with the persona and therefore establish that bridge of relationship.

5. Bring in safe environment of trust

You will know when someone doesn't feel safe, when there is awkwardness and distant body language. Hence why building a safe environment is important, without it a person can never open or be in a vulnerable state. Our focus and role is to make others feel safe and create a bond.

6. Honesty

Being a person of honesty brings out the authenticity of someone that is real and genuine. It cultivates relationships to make it easier to build trust.

7. Making sure others are heard

The most important skill to have is listening. Our main challenge is talking too much without doing any listening and understanding. Listening and active listening by connecting and paying attention shows the recipient that you are engaging.

8. First impression is your key to entrance

Making an entrance with impression does make an impact statement. People say first impressions last and I agree. It's the non-verbal language presence you bring. People are assessed through body language and the aesthetic appearance. So to improve your impression, straight back, shoulders relaxed, head up, chest firm and contagious genuine smile (not faking or obviously trying too hard). If you have open body language that you are not covering your body parts, crossed arms, people will view you subconsciously, open, friendly, and confident which people will respect.

9. Have your environment and people around you feel welcome and let your interactions be positive

Have you experienced feeling out of place around people who are not welcoming? It's because those types of people don't care about anyone except for their cliques.

If you want to be a great relationship builder, make people feel welcome by engaging, connecting and paying attention. Best way to connect is make them talk about themselves and just listen, this in turn gives them the sense of importance.

10. Zone relationships

In life we go through different types of relationships and we should allow learning, growth, and understanding to improve each relationship. The better the relationships you have, the better the quality of life you will have.

Your outlook and perspective will have a different type of lens when it comes to relationships. One thing to point out is to improve your relationships that are meaningful.

In relationships we go through a cycle and there are touchpoints we experience. In each area is where we take self-awareness to improve it.

Here are a few examples to get you thinking and start how you can take relationships to the next level.

Work and Business - Statistics says that 70% of our time is either spent at work or in business. This means the people that you work with are either enjoyable or not. So how do we improve relationship that leads success towards work and in business? Build rapport amongst each other and establish business connections that provides value in services and in products.

Partners or Spouse - We all know the importance of support, love, and connection. Sometimes it may not always be a bed of roses when faced with circumstances. It's through challenging times that partners and spouses are stronger than ever. Not everyone is the same in personality or in behaviors so it's important to know each other in depth. It takes time but it's worth it to know the intricate details of your significant other—their values, their mission, and their purpose. Each person has a responsibility in the relationship. So how do we improve the relationship? Build meaningful relationships with communication, experiences, and moments.

Family and Kids - If you have a family, you will know that there are challenging times to find that balance. Commitments and obligations can be strenuous to meet and the last thing in your mind is take rest whether it's from work or in business. Family I find to be the anchor, the motivation, the life towards one person. Family support and love is crucial in any relationship. Busyness can be the excuse for many people to make time for family. Most people value family as one of the most important values in life. How could you improve your family? What if you spend more time together? What if you bring them on a family trip experience? How about being home on time? Whatever it may be, find what ways you can create an environment of love, inspiration, and experiences. Life does pass by quickly and it's those memories that last forever.

Friends and colleagues – Oprah Winfrey quotes: "Surround yourself only with people who are going to lift you higher." I believe it's important to have friends and colleagues who believe in you but also speak truth when you need to hear it. Friends and associates can either influence positively or negatively which could lead you down a destructive path. I have seen it many times where one path can lead to a bright future and the other leads to darker path of no return. Hence why you need to choose your friends wisely. So how do you improve relationships? Build networks and connections that bring the experiences of a positive life. It doesn't matter how many they are, the important thing is that you are moving upwards and onwards in line with your true values.

THE SIMPLE ART OF HAPPINESS

The question we need to ask ourselves is, are we happy? The majority would say yes, others would say no, and the minority would be in the middle, still searching for what true happiness is.

Audrey Hepburn said: "The most important thing is to enjoy life – to be happy – it's all that matters."

Without being all spooky, airy fairy, and unrealistic towards the meaning of happiness, it's all about the simplicity around it that's not complicated.

It's a fact we all want to be happy, doing things that makes us happy, being around people that makes us happy, and thinking thoughts that makes us happy. What tends to happen when we're not self-aware is our circumstances and our emotions sometimes get the best of us.

It's easy to spend most of our thinking on negative thoughts because it's easy to fall into the trap. I believe happiness is a choice. Striving and being the best version of yourself with progress unleashes your happiness. The power of progression makes you happier. You see your personal journey and you're doing things that excites you.

We have an understanding of what happiness is and the question we need to ask ourselves is, are we happy? Are we living the life we truly deserve? This is where the negative mindset pops in and this is where you need to take action and replace it with an empowering self-belief. Don't let self-sabotage turn you away, because in reality you are more than enough and you are definitely stronger than you think.

I want to share five happiness insights that can change your life. This is what the internal success hacks are and that is to intentionally live a happier life. There is a saying: "Life's too short to live in misery, so live your best days now!"

When it comes to happiness you can experience it right now. There is plenty of perspectives about happiness. It's time we stop thinking of what life would be like instead of living the life now of what you do want. When you make the conscious effort of living intentionally for a happier life, this leads you to a meaningful purpose. Don't wait and say one day you will be happy, as most people tend to consciously think this. Be happy now and choose to make your thoughts positive.

FIVE WAYS OF HAPPINESS

Live your happiness

Think for a moment, when was the last time you said to yourself, "I'm going to live a happier life?" Was it months ago, years ago, days ago? The reason why I ask is so you can start thinking with intention and start taking action.

Earlier on I mentioned the power of potential that comes with two principles: self-awareness and responsibility. This also applies towards a happier life, being aware of your life, and taking ownership of your happiness. Being responsible for your personal happiness is actually your personal power. When you own it, that means you get to choose how you think, how you feel, and how you live it. This influences your positivity and outlook in life. What you see as a problem, challenge, or issue, you can turn it into a positive. You may feel it because we are all human, however, it never effects your positive state.

The happiness story

What you say about yourself and the stories that are created around it become a self-prophecy. Sometimes it's easy to stick to the narratives of self-pity and drama that is negative because it draws the persona of being a victim. When you change the way you think and talk about how you are destined for greatness, you will change your life.

Tony Robbins said: "Change your story, change your life. Divorce the story of limitation and marry the story of truth and everything changes."

If this quote resonates within you, then it's your time re-write your script and change the narrative of your life. Never let the past define you.

Enjoy your life now

We like to think in order to be happy we must reach a certain milestone, achieve something great, or becoming rich—then we can become happy. Sometimes we tend to be stressed with overwhelm and place limitation on thinking that good things never happen. It doesn't have to be that way, as we have learned that you can change your story and definitely change your life. In reality you don't need to do a certain activity to become happy. You can actually experience being happy right now. It's not a flip the switch type of thing, it's all about enjoying your personal journey and the entire process to wanting an epic life that includes celebrating along the way. Practicing gratitude is powerful and when you cultivate it as an attitude, you become happier.

Fulfilling relationships

Who we associate and surround ourselves with brings influence. It can either be good or bad and there's isn't anything between. Experiencing happiness is being intentional of the people you want to be with. If you know that the crowd you're with doesn't bring any value to your life, then it's best to make a decision for your future. When you know that the people that you have in your life bring joy, excitement, passion and positivity, then stick with them. You also want to contribute and add value to others, so that there is authenticity and connection, and that's what fulfilling relationships is all about. It's bringing out the best in all of us, moving steady in a direction together.

Make the balance

We can get caught up in life where we become very busy and not enjoy life where it matters. When you know you work hard, continuing to do the right things, this should also be balanced with play. I have seen people work hard and never reward themselves. This leads them in dissatisfaction with their passion that turns into a chore. It becomes 'I have to' rather than 'I want to.' Make the effort to bring in the balance so you can really experience the joy, happiness, and thrill when you know you are progressing.

Here are seven quick tips to activate your happiness:

1. *Contribution*

    Be the person that gives and contributes to the world. There isn't any greater feeling than to give out of love, compassion, and value.

2. *New skills*

    Learn new things as it creates creativity and fun. When you self-learn, it expands your personal value.

3. *Connection*

    Connect with like-minded people. This type of connection does bring out the best in you as you rub shoulders with other great people.

4. *Personal Goals*

    Set personal goals and celebrate your wins as this enhances your purpose and direction.

5. *Winning Attitude*

    Bring in your winning attitude, when life strikes you with circumstance, you become resilient with your actions.

6. *Positive Emotions*

    Have a positive outlook and experience joy, gratitude, and inspiration in creating an upward spiral.

7. *Self-worth*

    Knowing who you are with purpose-driven attributes brings in a whole different dimension toward your greatness.

ACTION STEPS

When your inner is empowered, your outer takes it to the next level.

- Why is it important to look after your inner and why?
- Has there been a time where you knew you can improve meaningful relationships in your life?
- List out your closest relationship that you want to invest your time into.
- How important is happiness to you and what do you do to make it fulfilling?
- What are the things you know that don't make you happy that you are currently tolerating, and what are the steps would you do to make yourself happy?

CHAPTER 10

CONQUER IN YOUR OUTER

"The meaning of life is not to simply to exist, to survive but to move ahead, to go up, to achieve, to conquer"
– Arnold Schwarzenegger

Now that you understand key insights to rise in your inner for success, we now need to unlock how you can conquer your outer for success.

In this chapter you will discover the other two of the four pillars of life, giving you the tools, foundation and steps towards your greatness. This is to encourage you to apply, test, and take action.

After many ups and downs, it has now worked for me. The aim is to go practical and not technical, moving you into action.

The purpose of this chapter is for you to take control of your health and wealth so you can improve your quality of life. When you feel great from within, it encourages you to take the lead, perform better, and look after your wellbeing with positivity. This type of habit will get you to see things in perspective when taking responsibility in making good choices towards your health and finance.

Our mindset is to see things in a positive resourceful way that is smart, quick, and efficient. In the real world this can be a challenge for many people. So how do we turn this around? We must acknowledge that there will be roadblocks, problems, and setbacks but this should not discourage you. Being prepared and self-aware gives you the advantage towards situations that will not deviate your goals and aspirations. Our true test is to ask ourselves how badly do we want to achieve our dreams and desires? How willing will you go the distance to fight through every adversity? What will it mean to you in fulfilling those things you have set in your mind, things that you wanted for your family, personal accolades and achievements? Then it's time to stir your drive and passion that enhances your intense focus of living an epic life of fulfilment.

Our DNA must come with realization to trust the process, embrace the journey, battle through adversity through failures, and still continue on. In fact many successful people have said that there are no shortcuts, which is true through experiences. It doesn't mean that it will stop you from learning, growing, improving, and modeling others of success. As an example, instead of experiencing five years of pain, learn from others so you don't have to go on the same path.

So what's next? In our previous chapter you have the power to rise in your inner state to empower your life externally. So what is the outer? It is your health and wealth, both providing significant impact towards your performance in life and business.

When you look after the external which is your health, you will start to rewire your mindset towards your financial wealth. There have been many research studies of the benefits in looking after your well-being that boosts your self-esteem, confidence, and performance.

I know from experience these two pillars were crucial for me. I had to reverse engineer my lifestyle. I went from external to internal—that means that when I started to change my physiology, I started to change my psychology. I then took notice of my entire life what I needed to improve and one of them was my finance.

> **I went from external to internal—that means that when I started to change my physiology, I started to change my psychology**

PILLAR OF HEALTH

If we truly want to experience a great life, our health is a priority. The challenges that are faced with poor health management can affect our energy, vitality, strength, and life span. It's not a good feeling being sick all the time. One of my values is health because it's the foundation for a good life. I know in Australia there a lot of people that want to lose weight and can't seem to shake it off because of their doubts, worries, and excuses.

Why do so many people find it hard to lose weight and achieve their health goals? Some say it's lack of belief, willpower, or self-esteem, or not enough affirmations.

It's simply not planning and taking action.

All it needs is a simple and achievable plan.

THRIVE AT FIVE

When you apply small steps incrementally you will experience the difference. It's like building a skyscraper—it takes time. It's not a pre-built framework and placing it on a commercial site. It doesn't happen that way. There's a saying: "Rome is not built in a day." Rome was eventually built in years, not days. When you make the habit of developing optimal health, it will help your mindset as well including your personal performance to achieving your goal.

How do we look after our health so it's not a yo-yo?

1. Be Specific and precise

What we have learned in goal setting is the exact same principle—be specific and in the present tense. Setup standards and rituals towards your health and fitness as an example.

- Eat healthy meals, not junk food
- Empty out bad and tempting food from the fridge
- Exercise daily

- Eat greens
- Avoid refined sugar and flour

If you want to use technology to keep on track, there are lot of applications in the marketplace. I'm not endorsing any products, however there are tools I use that keep me accountable. In terms of fitness I use Fitbit to track my steps and heart rate and Fitness Pal to track my food and calorie intake. I use www.Bodybuilding.com apps for my workout exercises.

2. Don't Give Up

When you start your journey and hit a roadblock, this is the time of testing. Don't give up. When you're on a mission, this is where you need to take a realistic approach and it's about building great habits. I remember when I first placed my details on my Fitness Pal app and noted my current levels of eating and activities. I wanted to lose 2 pounds per week. Automated ping notification corrected me and told me that I needed to lose 1 pound. So food for thought is don't place unrealistic plans that set yourself up to fail. Write out what you can do and achieve, then challenge yourself to the next level step by step.

3. Go for the long term success than the short sprint cookie cutter approach

We all want the shortcut six pack abs within a week. Though it sounds farfetched, we all want the fastest route. The only concern is that you can possibly head back to your old habits as fast as you have left them.

When you have a strong mind frame you will have a strong body frame. Looking toward the future that is focused on long term success will help you to keep at it. There are no quick fix. Focus on yourself to getting better every day. Make choices that give you the advantage. You want to enjoy your life, not deprive it. Choose to be smart when you eat and not indulge, knowing you'd regret it later.

4. Look at your goals and plan of action towards what you're eating

Meal prep and prepare your gym outfit. It may sound weird to you first but it will create great habits to your health success. Getting clear a day before or night before helps you start your day with a huge bang!

5. Fullproof your health by having an accountability buddy.

This is your anchoring success to continue your journey when you feel you want to give up and go back your normal life. Remember great things never happen in your comfort zone. Having an accountability buddy helps you stay accountable and responsible for your actions to make it happen. Your accountability buddy is there to kick your butt.

> **Remember great things never happen in your comfort zone**

COMBINING GREAT HEALTH AND WEALTH INTO OPTIMAL PERFORMANCES

Unlocking your greatness covers all aspects of life to being in control with your love, health, wealth, happiness, and your personal life. Wealth is an important discussion. I have seen relationships face problems when it comes to financial challenges. The purpose of wealth is to take control and action towards your finances. By taking responsibility in your finances, you will position yourself with opportunities.

I have seen instances where money can be a great thing that gives the lifestyle of what you want and there are other situations that finances can be very stressful. This section is to help you identify areas of where you need improvements and be self-aware of the mindsets you might have on money.

Financial debts and worries are the results of decisions made. Financial success and abundance are the outcomes of your choices from your mindset right through your strategies in wealth.

Right now you could be in any of these three different situations:

1. You're well off and have the freedom of money.
2. You're still getting there to your financial options and freedom.
3. You're struggling to live the lifestyle you want, and having challenges with financial circumstances.

I believe this third point is all backed by mindset, how you think, how you react, and what are your belief systems are about money.

When it comes to money, wealth, and prosperity, everyone has a different perspective about it. For some, others use it for self-gain, philanthropy, security, power, influence, control etc. There isn't any universal scale of how much money is really enough. You can be the wealthiest person and yet have poor health, only days to live, or could be financially secure and your relationships around you are suffering. It may sound crazy to think that and most people are not satisfied. The most important thing to know is, are you fulfilled? Are you experiencing fulfilment in what you do? Are you happy?

The first step for a healthy financial management strategy is to know where you stand currently. The thinking, guess work, and the pondering won't work.

If you tell yourself it's too hard to go into the details or choose to ignore it or have different set beliefs about it and if it's not serving you in a positive way, then it's time to re-think with a new strategy. This could mean that you are maybe spending more than you earn, not tracking your expenses, choosing wants over what is needed, and failing to save or invest.

Nothing will ever change in your current circumstance if you don't face the reality and look at your current habits, strategies, and choices you currently make. Try to understand what has not worked and why it has resulted that way. Accepting your current ways are not good enough. Be honest to yourself.

Why are your finances and health important in conquering your outer? Because it gives you the flexibility and freedom to giving back and adding more value in your life and the people around you.

So now that you have your health in checked, let's look into ways to conquering your finances so you can have your four pillars of life such as love, happiness, health, and wealth catapult you into greater heights for success.

Remember success is not just about money, it's about everything in moving and thriving forward.

7 WAYS TO JUMPSTART THE FINANCIAL JOURNEY

Little disclaimer: Achieving financial breakthrough and freedom takes time, which is not a sprint but a journey. It is always said that the wealthiest people develop a habit of getting wealthy slow rather than getting rich very quickly.

Note: Consistency is key.

As you have unlocked parts of the financial route, go through this section with full intention and concentration. Adapt and absorb the content and complete the action steps. Take advantage of this chapter to set your goals and reframe your mind for financial success.

Step 1 – Mindset

If you truly want to live an abundant life, then the requirement is that you need to act and think like a person who is abundant specifically in the area of wealth. Believe, think, and act like a successful person.

It may sound funny to hear for the first time, it is said you are what you believe.

The challenge is that it's not enough to just think it and therefore you are given it on a silver platter. What is required in the process is hard work, smart strategies, and endless pursuit of hunger to achieve any kind of success. This all begins by taking and accepting full responsibility of your current financial circumstances, the ups and the downs, the good and the ugly. You have the power to make the change. I know for myself when I used to be in huge credit card debt, I paid the minimal amount and really didn't care.

If you're experiencing that same feeling, then it's time to face the facts and do something about it. You don't need to be scared and feel you have lost—you have every power within you to beat your financial challenges.

It's time you remove the poverty mindset of "I can't" into an empowering mindset of "I can!" Once you start thinking at a different level as being a successful person, you will start to manifest with your actions. Being broke, poor, scared, and stressed is only temporal and not the end result, because you have the opportunity right now to turn it around into your favor.

Step 2 – Time to budget and do the little things

Every successful person knows the inside details of what goes in and what goes out. This is the practised skill we need to have that separates us from being financially poor to being financially successful. Knowing where your funds go is crucial for your budgeting and financial goals you have set.

There are two practical little things which is a significant thing to get started.

1. Spend less than you earn

This step could be a challenge for others, especially if you live by paycheck to paycheck, spending without thinking. This insight to spend less can assist you to increase your money and save significantly. Instead of paying any type of expenses, its best to pay yourself first (very important – auto debit it) Also important that this goes to a specific investment like separate savings account or managed funds that way it is not spent - you can start by 5% to 10%. Avoid leaving the leftovers for savings. Start to build great habits and make that commitment to give 10% of what you earn into your savings and investments so it can grow. I see this as an analogy—plant a seed and it will grow.

Be encouraged to do a budget. Communicate to all parties of your household so everyone is on board and accountable. A good book on this is the barefoot investor.

2. Cut out the credit card spending habit

Credit cards are only handy when it is spent wisely and returned immediately. Most people think credit cards are free money. It could feel that way, only to bite you back on the bum when you have to pay it back. Credit cards are dead money that give you more interest and nothing in return. The pain it will cause in the end if you're late in repayments and can't pay feels terrible. And what's even worse is to pay off that credit card with another credit card.

So right now if you are experiencing this pain, identify your pattern and reverse engineer it. You are in a pathway you think you cannot get out. Let me tell you that you can get out of it. Take a stand and the stop the credit card madness. One of the keys to success is to spend less than you earn.

Step 3 – Finding your passion

There is a favorite quote from TD Jakes which says, "Your passion will lead you right in your purpose." So the question we need to ask ourselves is, "What kind of difference can I make for my life and others?" It's combining purpose and passion together.

Purpose-driven people follow their passion, but it's more than just passion itself, it's the power of clarity. Being clear of the direction influences your clarity into knowing your mission of who you are, what you really want and where you are going. It is setting your goals and achieving those goals and making those plans into a reality. When you create and accomplish the milestones you've set and progress through it, this will build more confidence and empower your self-belief. It reinforces your mindset that anything is possible, that the limits are actually limitless.

The passion that you have needs to come with specifics and clarity. When you move toward it, this gives you the drive to action and clear the pathway of your financial breakthrough.

Step 4 – Motivation

It's possible to lose focus, motivation, and inspiration at times. So how do we stay constantly motivated and inspired? You have to ask yourself provoking, invoking questions that stir you like: What is your why and what are your reasons?

Step 5 – Improve your career

Always remember that people look out for themselves. It doesn't mean people don't care about you, it's that people do things for themselves first before others.

When it comes to your career, don't be stagnant to where you are. In fact, the future is bright to those who step up, ask what they want, and do what it takes to bridge any gaps in their career. If you want to increase your salary rate, you must do one crucial thing and that is to be a person of high value.

So how do we do this? If there's a high-paying role or opportunity then ask management what the gaps are that they need to improve to get ahead? Get clarity and direction if you want an increase of pay with the financial freedom of flexibility. Put a case together, write out your plan of action, and be strategic in how you can do that. Make a list of roles and write out what additional skills you have to acquire. Start thinking what highlights and achievements you have accomplished to increase your value.

Utilize the Kaizen approach which is to continuously improve. Learn related topics that can help give you the edge. Always add value to yourself and your situation and to your clients.

Step 6 – Take entrepreneurship seriously

Starting a business or being in business can be challenging and exciting at the same time. There has been a lot said that you get the luxury of choosing your own times of operations, and being your own boss. It's not a bed of roses when it comes to entrepreneurship. You have to work hard, be smart, follow your passion and drive, and treat customers as number one.

Place more effort and time to improve and be the forefront over your competition. You will exceed and succeed.

You do not get rich by working for someone else. You must have an entrepreneurial mindset, even if you just work at a supermarket but invest in other ways on the side. See it as if you are running an investment business because it is through these activities of investments you can achieve financial freedom.

If you're not running your own business then shift your thinking that your savings and investments are your business.

Step 7 – The power of Compounding

For every little step forward makes a significant difference in the overall picture.

The compounding principle is all about the process where the value of earnings of an investment increases which interests are earned through time. What this means that growth occurs whatever you earn in the form of interest which could be payments, return on investments, dividends, bonuses, all your earnings above your expected monthly amount.

Compounding is an opportunity to create wealth by investing. You need to become an investor and invest, and in due time will see the growth during the process.

Let it be today and the rest of your life that you take control of your financial status. If you are thinking of investing, seek a professional advisor.

Here are learning tips I received when I sought a professional:

Learn leveraging – Use other people's money to make money, maybe bank's money or your investors' money. Good use of leverage can exponentially elevate your wealth.

Learn also diversification – Do not put your eggs all in one basket. Also do not rely on just one means of income. Look at establishing multiple streams of income. There are a lot books on this topic, especially the book *Multiple Streams of Income,* which you can reference.

Step 8 – Learn, grow and have a role model

Be a student and learn the foundation of finance because you will start to feel you are in control of your life. Have a role model, align your beliefs to those who are successful and have earned to what you want to earn. Be a constant learner.

It's important to be in an environment that is the right environment for your life. There will always be people who have earned a significant amount of money who are successful, so make the effort and energy to be in the same room. This could be in women's and/or men's networks, business clubs, meet-ups, wealth groups, seminars and workshops. Having a buddy or mentor will help in providing accountability and guidance. Stay humble and feet planted. Don't forget where you came from as you succeed. Learn to give, and be blessed to be able to bless others.

QUICK TIPS

Be persistent. You can start in reading financial self-help books or seek an advisor. There are a lot of options and be the person of curiosity to get you closer to your goals and aspirations. What separates unsuccessful people and successful people who are millionaires is that they acted upon on it with urgency. Most millionaires are self-made millionaires. They started from the bottom, just like everybody else, but it did not stop them in fighting and achieving their dreams. We need to be same, having the same drive and passion.

Finding and following their formula will get the same results. Aligning belief systems will give a different mindset such as money is the root of all evil or you can be financially abundant. I had poor belief systems about money and it did not serve me well, not until I made the decision to change. When you earn money you have the control of your finances, and it's your choice what you do with it.

ACTION STEPS

All it takes is your decision to be the best version of yourself. When you take ownership for your life through health and finance everything will follow with success. When your outer is empowered, everything is a following affect with success.

- What do you need to do now to improve your current health?
- Identify your bad habits toward health and list out what you can do now to create good habits.
- What type of mindsets do you have toward your health and wealth?
- Where are you currently in your financial status?
- What are the steps you can implement that will help you in your financial journey?

CHAPTER 11

BE THE BIGGER PERSON

"We make a living by what we get, but we make a life by what we give."
– Winston Churchill

Have you heard of the saying, "Give and you shall receive?" I tend to ponder this a lot and I'm curious when reading books on self-development and being mentored by successful people that one of the ingredients for continuing success is contribution. I find that the attributes towards successful people is that they live and breathe in giving that doesn't expect anything in return.

However, the principle of giving comes back in double folds. I see this as an analogy that as we open our hands to give whatever you can—whether it's providing value, helping others, or contributing towards a worthy cause—that because your hands open they are free to receive. If it's the opposite where we give with our closed fists, in return we cannot receive.

As a farmer if you continue to fertilize, look after the soil, and invest in the nutrients by sowing and watering the seed, it will grow significantly. In other words, if you invest your life in others or causes, that's bigger than yourself and it definitely gives you that internal fulfilment.

POWER OF GIVING

A life of giving and contribution to others is an indescribable feeling. It's a way where it brings significant purpose that moves you from focusing onto yourself to others, it's a different type of perspective.

Be the bigger person towards contribution. Ben Carson quotes "Happiness doesn't result from what we get, but from what we give."

So how do we shift our mindset to becoming a giver where we feel there isn't much to give? I have this dilemma all the time and much of it is towards money. You may feel the same way, and this is where the magic happens. Giving is not just about only money as this is the easiest excuse to bring up. It's your time, energy, and efforts toward contribution that matters. When you shift your mindset toward purpose and adding so much value, then money and other means of resources will not be an issue. Whether it's small or big, you should do everything you can to make a difference in this world.

Live an epic life by unleashing greatness that is driven with purpose, motivation and inspiration. When you do good things to this world and others, you will attract the same abundance in return. We all want to be successful in every area of our lives and it's the law of cause and effect—we sow and we will reap.

I remember many years ago when I started to give. I wasn't really well off with my finance in my early twenties. I had the mentality to spend more than I earned and whenever I made money, I would squander it. One thing that really struck a chord within me is supporting families in the third world countries through charities and mission work.

There have been many times I've been tested to give more and not to think about myself and it was only then I started to feel I was making an impact in the life others who are less fortunate. It was that moment that I didn't have to worry and was experiencing internal abundance without any lack. When you are in control of your finances and not being controlled by it, you find freedom that will not hold you back.

So how do we improve our lives towards contribution?

1. Understanding the power of value and giving
2. Taking responsibility to learn, grow, and develop
3. Focus on value and add value to others
4. Empower to give and influence others

UNDERSTANDING THE POWER OF VALUE AND GIVING

I believe that placing goals, achieving your dreams, and taking action is something people can do it with excellence. When it comes to giving, whether it's your time, resources and money, this is where the rubber meets the road. Many successful people have this in their mindset and their secret is giving more to a worthy cause that provides significant difference in the world.

They understand that wealth that is earned is not for taking, it is for giving. We tend to think that to give is all about money, and in fact that's not the case, it's really your time, resources and the value you give. Money is also a factor, however, it is giving yourself. You have the power and opportunity to turn difficult situations into better solutions.

Giving back to your community and other people that may need your help or being a mentor unveils your mission on what you're made for. Focusing on others has a generating spark plug that ignites and motivates you to do more and do things above and beyond.

This type of mindset gives you purpose, meaning, and definitely fulfilment. What you sow, you will reap and the benefits become evident. You become more passionate and more productive to find more ways to create solutions to problems. This sense of inner value will overcome any overwhelm and exhaustion because there is strength when your focus is not yourself. When we contribute back to people with a positive attitude, it comes with impact and the result of this we become bigger than ourselves.

TAKING RESPONSIBILITY TO LEARN, GROW, EXPAND, AND DEVELOP

For people to grow and expand their potential, we must grow first. If we are to be a person of value to others then we must invest in ourselves to be effective, efficient, and focused.

Personal development is the key for exponential success and there is an interesting pattern that all successful people have—most importantly, how consistent they are when it comes to their greatness. Learning and growing is key.

Whenever I coach my clients I always ask this question: "What do you think the greatest investment may be?" The first thing I hear is shares, stocks, bonds, properties, and businesses—all relating to money. There's nothing wrong with the investment in terms of money, but I believe it's deeper and more meaningful towards investment.

When it comes to investment, everyone has different ideas, methods, and philosophies. The true investment that I'm referring to is not purely about money. It is actually greater than money itself. It is the person you are that brings internal value into substance.

I want you to pause for a minute and visualize the best value you can bring that results in significant return. Now you're wondering what possibly could be the greatest investment of all time. Is it property? Is it shares? Is it business ventures and partnerships? The answer is personal development. It is investing in yourself with the wealth of knowledge to becoming the best person you can be in adding so much value into your life and others.

You are the greatest asset, the greatness that resides in you has so much empowering potential to creating transformational change of success. You have been given an opportunity of choice and decision, and it's up to you to make it happen. It's a wonderful thing to know you can achieve anything.

Just imagine without the personal development where would inspiration, motivation and innovation come from? Personal development gives you access to unlocking greater awareness of areas to improve, get better and be effective, because it is the confidence that you gain when you invest in yourself with books, seminars, workshops, impacting networks and trainings that will assist your gifts and strengths to the next level.

Henry Ford said, "Anyone who stops learning is old, whether at twenty or eighty. Anyone who keeps learning stays young." I have read this quote numerous times and what pops into my mind is when you are constantly learning, you are growing and expanding. This means that by being young, as an attribute you have a burning desire, enthusiasm, and a fire within to take the leaps and bounds of faith into action. Have you ever wondered why the elderly couples who have been married for decades are called Young at Heart? It's because they still have that same burning desire of love for one another!

So how does that relate to the greatest investment?

Learning and growing enhances and heightens your personal development to be at its cutting edge. Learning gives you drive and energy as it opens your mind to the possibility of creativity. This is why successful entrepreneurs, business owners, CEOs, leaders, and influential personnel are always optimistic as they are well informed and constantly inputting valuable insights in their repertoire to improve.

Brian Tracy who is a success expert coach says, "Personal Development is your springboard to personal excellence. Ongoing, continuous, non-stop personal development literally assures you that there is no limit to what you can accomplish." If you can reread this 4-5 times over there is no limit to what you can accomplish when personal development becomes part of your life's journey.

FOCUS ON VALUE AND ADD VALUE TO OTHERS

So many successful people are all about value and what's important to them is how it can serve others in any shape, way, or form. It's about creating meaning in your life that is not what you do for yourself, it's how you can improve other people's lives. In reality it's not what you get, it's what you give that creates meaning.

How do we create that meaning? There are three simple steps:

1. Find Your Drive

What motivates you internally in life? What are the things you really enjoy and feel that sense of accomplishment? Why do you enjoy making money? Is it for your family, or is it for personal achievements? Do you enjoy making contributions to your work and company? For every action you make comes with intention and purpose.

2. Do it in smaller steps

One of the setbacks that most people tend to think is that they feel that don't have enough to give. However they have a lot to give that doesn't relate to money, it's the time, energy and effort to contribute. By starting small and taking action now will transform your mindset that will enable you to contribute.

3. Start a tsunami wave

Before a tsunami ever gets created it comes with a disruption. You are disrupting to create an impact. Some of the most notable people, to name a few, are Mark Zuckerberg and Bill Gates. Despite immeasurable wealth, they make ways to make a positive impact towards their action to make a difference around the world. I believe you can create a ripple effect with your attitude, behavior, belief and contribution. You will feel internal joy that fills your soul through your giving.

EMPOWER TO GIVE AND INFLUENCE OTHERS

Greatness is not just about getting or achieving key milestones, it's all about giving and making significant difference.

Seeing greatness in others is another way to give back.

ACTION **STEPS**

Your super hero abilities is the power of contribution and you make the difference when you take action.

- What would be your first contribution if you have the time, energy and money?
- How has giving and supporting others helped you in your journey toward greatness?
- Have there been areas of lack you want to improve on? What are they?
- What are the insights you want to take onboard that you can build as a habit in giving?
- What is your mantra in life?

CHAPTER 12

FOLLOW THROUGH IN ACTION

"Words may inspire but only action creates change."
– Simon Sinek

We've all heard that action is the key to success. Pablo Picasso said famously, "Action is the foundational key to all success." In essence, I find it to be true. The only dilemma is I've noticed that taking action will take you to your destination, however there is more. What I mean, before any reader goes into defense mode and says, "Gez, you're kidding right?" is that taking action is more than enough in my eyes.

Well, let's go deeper. I know everyone has a certain particular dream that they want to fulfil. A goal that they eagerly want to achieve that brings significant value. The question that comes to mind is, how long have we been thinking about this? Are we actually doing something about it? Are we getting closer to achieving it? No matter what excuses are in the bag, complete ownership is required in our lives.

This chapter is to help you see the complete picture in what you have learned from all the chapters. It is the follow through in taking action and constantly moving forward to improve and achieve with excellence non-stop.

There are three categories that we potentially may fall into:

1. Procrastinators
2. Thinkers
3. Doers

CHAMPION MENTALITY

I believe that there is more to just taking action. There needs to be a 'champion mentality' to execute, follow through, and improve as a repeated cycle. I'm not just talking about winning in sports or any of that kind. It's the mindset of the right precision of execution towards action. Connor McGregor UFC Champion says it perfectly: *"Precision beats power and timing beats speed."*

So here's the punchline: "Action is not good, it's the level of intensity you need to bring throughout the action from start to finish including follow-through that it becomes great."

Connor McGregor can come with plenty of words, however, he backs it up by training intensely hard behind the scenes. I'm not referring to the physical challenges, I'm referring on the mindset he brings that he conditions his mind frame as a champion, a victor, and a conqueror. This is the type of tenacity we need to bring when it comes to greatness. That mind frame must be rewired to be successful no matter what the circumstances may come your way.

I have seen, coached, workshopped and spoken even on stage where I hear stories that people took action but did not follow through. It made me wonder, have I ever taken action but never followed through? I started to get real curious as to what beliefs I had that stopped my progression through action? Then I came to realize that I had these excuses in my mind:

"This is not going to work."
"I have failed so many times."
"People will think of me differently."
"I'm not good enough."
"I know what the result will be anyway, so I won't give it my best."

Does this sound familiar? Have you felt that way before, with excuses upon excuses in your head that don't encourage you to proceed any further? Have you experienced where you did something but you made a condition in your mind that it's going to suck even before you started in taking action? Then the self-prophecy came to pass and it sucked? You are not alone on this.

GET INTO ACTION MODE

In order to achieve great results in your life is to stay in a positive state that means after you have taken action is that you follow through. Just like in boxing when your opponent gets clipped by your uppercut punch and is completely dizzy, you go for the knockout punch for the win. This type of attitude when it comes to greatness that you don't go half way to your goals, you go all the way. We should never settle for less and play it halfheartedly. The reason as to why we follow through is important because it encourages us to take action without any fear or doubts. This in fact leads to constant improvements to getting better every single time you take action. When you start achieving your goals, you get excited and then sometimes you stop. In order to avoid being stagnant and hit the ceiling, reflection and projection is key. This means you reflect what you have done—both challenges and opportunities—during the entire process. You project what you can do better and implement the improvements. Why do we see champions accomplish greater things? Because once they conquer something, they want to challenge themselves to the next level. This is the type of mentality we need to have, because motivation is not an airy fairy feeling, it's a commitment and determination without the hype in achieving greater things and living your epic life you always wanted.

So how do we do it? How do we turn ourselves from procrastinators into doers? Get yourself organized, visualize your future of success, and tell yourself that you are the champion for this, making a commitment to yourself, eliminating distractions, building accountability, and go in daily with a plan and action.

FIVE KEYS TO TAKE ACTION TO ANOTHER LEVEL

Key 1 – Intensity

Come with a game plan of intensity every time you are going to take action with a detailed plan of attack.

Key 2 – Feedback

When things don't go your way and someone critiques you or criticizes you, don't take it personally. Take it as feedback and re-frame your mind that failure is not failure it's only feedback to getting better and smarter.

Key 3 – Relentless

If you have a huge why to achieve something great, whether it's your dreams, goals, aspiration both in life and in business, then be relentless! Never stop and never give up.

Key 4 – Follow-through

Action is powerful with an empowered follow-through. Be bigger than your circumstance or situation because there will always be hurdles and resistance. Do what you say and say what you do, always follow through and deliver – WARNING: Do not wait, wish, and hope! Because you will stay there forever.

Key 5 – Appreciation

Attitude of gratitude is a very popular saying. However, it has so much meaning to it. We can get caught in the moment of stressful expectations, just turn it into appreciation. Be grateful and have an attitude to always give, have an outlet where you can provide value to others.

So right now take the challenge and make this year the best year ever by taking your action to another level. Bring in your A-Game because you deserve the best life. These insights may be a reminder, a wake-up call, or plainly a kick in a butt. So continue to be resilient in your approach and constantly stay hungry toward success and do what you are destined and called to do – live life of fulfilment.

DEVELOP A RESOUNDING HUNGER

Motivation and action are the result of your focus and hunger. Every four years the world stops when the Olympics are on. Whenever this event is on and I'm watching the television, I'm always fascinated to see just how many people represent their country with such pride and honor. We are not consciously aware at times about what goes on behind the scenes. Every athlete comes with a story and what it means to be on the Olympic stage. Can you imagine what it feels like to be representing your own country? Or the feeling that you have qualified to be competing at the highest level of your life? Or the journey you went through to get in? There's a lot of mixed emotions that happens in the Olympics and the kind of preparation and process that each athlete goes through.

What inspires the athletes what really transpires into in what they do best? What is that hidden driver that makes them so elite that they are able to grind it out day in and day out with sweat, blood and tears running through them? Is it the talent? Is it the knowledge? Is it the connection? Is it their gifts? I would say it is hunger!

I believe to achieve greatness in our personal lives we all need that type of hunger to press on and not give up on what we want in life.

Having a hunger will make you achieve no matter what happens in your life. Here is an insight of hunger if you activate and apply it right now. What initiates an empowered life? It is your internal hunger translated into intense focus of achievement and fulfilment.

FIVE THINGS THAT HUNGER DOES TO AWAKEN THE GREATNESS IN YOU:

1. Hunger brings out the best in you
2. Hunger brings your life to the next level
3. Hunger brings focus to execute
4. Hunger brings your vision to life
5. Hunger brings an attitude to not give up till you reach your goals

These five are powerful insights and I encourage you right now to get back that hunger. The hungrier you are the more focused and determined you are to take action and thrive forward.

What brings your hunger is your inner why, knowing that you have a purpose and mission. When you know that everything inside you brings fulfilment, you become more purposeful in your passion.

After you have followed through with action, always keep in mind that you are enough and made for greatness. The opportunities and possibilities are there for you, combining that champion mentality makes you more than enough for success.

I AM ENOUGH

How do we remind ourselves that we are more than enough, even when faced with challenges? We need three perspectives.

1. Inner Self-Belief
2. No Failure Only Step Forward
3. Dare to Dream

Inner Self-Belief

We need inner self-belief and I'm not referring to religious belief. What I'm pointing out is how much belief do you have in yourself? These attributes of confidence, enthusiasm, grit, hustle, hunger, passion, and purpose are your key strengths to empowering your self-belief. Never allow circumstances, situations, or setbacks be the culprit in affecting your confidence in what you want in life. Continue to speak positive affirmations over your life even when you don't feel like it. Be the person of courage, do the things that energizes you with passion and you'll experience what you have envisioned for your life.

No Failure, Only Step Forward

Mistakes and constant failures are inevitable. Acknowledging it is your step forward. When you develop learning habits with action then mistakes, mishaps and failures are a good thing. You will learn, grow, and improve at the same time. You are an inch closer to perfection, per se. If you think about the Wright Brothers, Orville and Wilbur Wright, who were the American aviators who built the first ever flying airplane. Can you imagine all the setbacks they experienced and hardships they would've faced? Think about all the resources, time, energy, and effort spent? And yet they still continued on because of their passion, drive, and vision to make it into reality. The Wright brothers did not stop till they reached success. So in life don't take failure as ultimate failure, take it as feedback to improve and succeed.

Dare to Dream

Dreamers who are action-takers will not be satisfied for second best. In fact, they take the leap of faith, audaciously daring and be purposely out of their comfort zone. There's a four step acronym towards your dream that inspires your greatness.

(D) *Determination* — Have a positive attitude of determination that is focused and unwavering. Be the person that is unstoppable.

(R) *Responsibility* — Take ownership of your life and be responsible for every action you take. Be the person that lives life on your terms.

(E) *Education* — Your personal development unlocks the wisdom, knowledge, and insights you need for success. Be the person that is relentless towards learning.

(A) *Attitude* — Your attitude with your gratitude brings you fulfilment, it gives you a different perspective of "I can, I will, I must" factor. Be the person of influence.

(M) *Motivation* — When you are purpose-driven, motivation is no longer a chore, it's a lifestyle. Be the person that hones in to your goals, dreams and aspiration.

IN CLOSING

These insights are more tools you have in your toolkit that best prepare you for anything. You are destined for greatness and the motivation that's within you is not hype, it's for real.

Combining everything that you have learnt covered you from end to end. The next steps are for you to apply the principles, then change the strategies to make it work for you.

Be the person to evolve to be the best human ever that thrives on challenges and conquers any limitation. I believe in you and you can achieve what you think is impossible because you are stronger, smarter, and more inspiring than you think.

ACTION STEPS

Action with the follow through mechanism helps you, elevates your game plan and unleashes your greatness.

- What types of strategies would you implement to follow through better?
- What category do you fall into – Procrastinator, Thinker, or Doer? What would you need to do to improve?
- How would you unleash your hunger for success? Why?
- What is your current inner self-belief? Is it empowering or disempowering, and why?
- Which insights in this chapter really resonated in you to take action?

CHAPTER 13

21 DAYS OF THRIVE CHALLENGE

WHAT IS 21 DAYS OF THRIVE?

I know most people love short, sweet, and straight to the point. This challenge is like no other. It's concise with intention and short motivational messages for 21 days, tailor made for a busy lifestyle. This means it leaves out all the excuses of not having the time.

How does it feel to be encouraged by your loved one, partner, spouse, work colleague, or your boss which gives you that extra little boost? Doesn't it make your day and create that internal feeling that you have conquered the world? Twenty-one Days of Thrive is purposely fitted for this. It focuses on 21 impacting words to empower and fuel your passion in life. It is a way to improve daily and change your mindset to be a better version of yourself.

What are the 2 keys to unlock 21 days of Thrive?

1. Apply
2. Activate

It's that simple! We human beings like to complicate things all it requires is ACTION.

Why do the 21 Days of Thrive Challenge?

People say it takes at least 40 - 66 days to change a habit. What if you were up for the challenge to do it in 21 days with absolute focus and determination?

The key is consistency, and it's about making a decision through your thoughts and taking action.

How does 21 Days of Thrive work?

Each day you will read one of the motivational messages from the 21 Days of Thrive. You will evaluate and decide to improve on your personal life. When it comes to power of affirmation, make sure to shout out loud and visualize your personal success. The words you say to yourself will shape your destiny, and when you have empowering language, you will start to notice transformative changes.

Take the challenge and your 21 days will epically change your life!

DAY 1
MOMENTUM – STEAM TRAIN

When you think about momentum the perfect example will be a steam train, its power is pulled through a steam engine using coal, wood, or oil. As it burns the fuel, steam pushes the train through the rail tracks. The more materials are put into the steam engine, the more power it generates. The momentum it gives is enormous which thrusts its force to move forward. When you want to achieve great things in your life, do not be discouraged because you are not there yet, every force you need is to not give up on pursuing it till you get it. Fight it through as you fuel up your goals, desires, dreams, and aspirations. It will provide momentum you are striving for.

Power of Affirmation

"Momentum gets me moving precisely to what I want to achieve in life. I CAN, I WILL, I MUST!"

DAY 2
OPPORTUNITIES – BEHIND THE SITUATION

Opportunities can be viewed in 3 different ways when we suddenly hit a brick wall called problems, setbacks, and obstacles. Have you ever come across a situation where you felt you missed out on the great things in life? Or you just made a decision that you shouldn't have taken and the outcome did not result in your favor?

You are not alone. What if you were to view these situations from a different perspective where the opportunities are hidden behind the problem, setbacks and obstacles? All it requires is to learn, strategize, and execute better ways because it is an opportunity to rise above it, to grow, and have personal strength to carry on.

Power of Affirmation

*"Opportunities are always around me.
I have the power to seize the moment
and go towards it
I CAN, I WILL, I MUST!"*

DAY 3
HEALTH – IS EVERYTHING

Vitality and having great health is so important. Without it, the implications will cause serious health issues and significant weight gain, which can be detrimental to your lifestyle. We all know that we need to eat healthy food and regularly exercise which is one of the foundations of vitality. The only dilemma we face is the first things we tell ourselves is, "I'm too busy, buying food is too expensive, I'd hate to change my diet."

If we take out the excuses to make a change, all it requires is a step by step, day by day approach making healthy choices daily. Always remember the foundational steps – always think positively, eat often with great nutritional food, exercise consistently, get good rest, and drink plenty of water. So decide and commit now to having a healthy lifestyle. It is never too late, so start planning and start doing.

Power of Affirmation

"I have everything in my ability to live a healthy lifestyle that gives me happiness and energy.
I CAN, I WILL, I MUST!"

DAY 4
GRATEFUL – IN THE SIMPLE THINGS

Grateful is one of the key word to a quality life; it means a deep appreciation of the act of kindness and the warmth of thankfulness. We all have moments of frustrations, pains, setbacks, stress, and overwhelming situations that it takes over our emotions. Have you ever experienced a time where you took the time to cool down and it resulted in clearing your mind. It made you realize that it wasn't that bad. As you start to be grateful you realize that other people in the world have experienced much worse conditions. Be thankful and be grateful in the life that you have, and the opportunity and power to be a better person.

Power of Affirmation

"Being grateful helps me and my attitude to be appreciative in life. I CAN, I WILL, I MUST!"

DAY 5
AWESOME – OF THOUGHTS

The word awesome has a lot interpretations and it does have an impact in how we use it. What if were to say that you were awesome and that you can do awesome things? We never think of ourselves being that awesome, but what if you did? How would that feel? Wouldn't that just make your day? One of those feelings is getting things done, ticking off the boxes on your to do list, going after something and receiving it – it is the sense of small, medium or big things of achievement, which is called ACTION. Being awesome is being a person of action, saying the things you will do, and doing the things you say. Whatever your mission in life is, be that person of awesome because awesome things happen to awesome people.

Power of Affirmation

"I am that awesome I was called to BE. I CAN, I WILL, I MUST!"

DAY 6
COURAGE – IS YOUR WEAPON FOR FEAR

There are 3 things to fear that we all have experienced at one point in our lives. The fears that we are facing now, the fears that we can manage, and the fears we know we have conquered. Can you remember a time when you were afraid of something, but all you did was go for it? All of a sudden you felt happy, invincible, and confident to take up the next challenge. When you feel stuck and paralyzed, how do you push through? Your weapon is courage. This only happens when you take action! If you are fearful that you cannot succeed or people say you can't make it in life, all you need is courage to do whatever it takes to action, as you are more courageous than you think.

Power of Affirmation

"I have courage, I am victorious, and fear cannot stop me because I rise above my fears through my courage. I CAN, I WILL, I MUST!"

DAY 7
VISION – YOUR SUCCESS

Every great leader and every successful person has a vision. They are captured with intense focus which they share a common visual eye. This means they have their sight set heading towards a direction they see coming to pass. No matter what happens or things that come their way, they are driven by their constant vision. What they place in their mind daily, and what they've written down to do. It is that 'attitude vision' that comes to reality. You may be thinking, can I possibly have that attitude vision that will come to pass? The answer is yes! Right now be purposeful with intent in what vision you want for your life. Write it, speak it, and live it. You have what it takes to take your vision to the next level.

Power of Affirmation

"It is not defined by how long or how far the vision is, it is defined by how much passion, pursuit, and process it takes to relentlessly to achieve it. I CAN, I WILL, I MUST!"

DAY 8
CHAMPION – WITH A CAUSE

Heart of a champion brings discipline, grit, toughness, a never giving up attitude, willpower, resolve, and determination. All these elements have been used one way or the other to bring great strength of character. Whether the person wins or loses, this nature of life does not dictate or define a person. It empowers the individual to move forward and do it again. It is the mentality of a champion to master their skill and rise above challenges. I believe every individual has a heart of a champion. All it requires is a decision, discipline, and that fire to get up the next morning to chase your dreams. A spirit to fight for your goals, and to breakthrough limiting mindsets. Bring that fight in you, to have an epically awesome life you deserve. It's not easy being a champion, but it is worth the blood, sweat, and tears to achieve it.

Power of Affirmation

*"I am a champion, I have a heart of champion, I have made my decision, and my time is now.
I CAN, I WILL, I MUST!"*

DAY 9
PASSION – THAT GIVES YOU THE OOMPH

The word passion tells it all. It is a strong emotion that compels, drives, and pushes. It is such a great force that it will move you. Have you ever met a relative, friend, colleague that is passionate about something, and all they do is rave about their passion non-stop? Ever wondered what it would be like to do the same, doing the things you love and turning your passion to profit? So how do we turn up our passion? By being self-aware of your life, evaluating yourself, and evaluate what excites you about life. What is your ambition? What are your hobbies? What activities give you fulfilment and satisfaction? Answering these questions can encourage you to let the passion give you the zest to enjoy the life you deserve.

Power of Affirmation

"I will do what I'm passionate about in the things of life and I refuse to let it die. I CAN, I WILL, I MUST!"

DAY 10
INSPIRE – GREATNESS

Being inspired is an incredible feeling, and inspiring is even better! Have you experienced a situation when someone approached you for help, and you provided assistance, and they said thank you with sincerity? Or a time when you volunteered and lend a helping hand that made an impact in someone's life that changed their world for the better? All you were thinking is that you have become a superhero, saving the day, and felt on top of the world. Whether it is large or small, you can make a difference by inspiring others that needs your encouragement, faith, and belief that they can also live a life of greatness. Having an attitude of gratitude to give and sow in different forms of contribution can really put everything into perspective that you have the power to inspire and empower someone.

Power of Affirmation

*"I'm inspired to inspire others.
I CAN, I WILL, I MUST!"*

DAY 11
COMMITMENT – TO STAY ON COURSE

When a decision is made, a follow-through of that decision is a commitment. We all know that for most people, commitment is a strong word because it is an agreement to what you are going to do. It is a word that transforms your journey into reality. We don't see and enter the promise land just by thinking and questioning. A commitment is a solid decision combined with action that will get you to the fulfilment of your goals. It is the driving force for your personal success. Nothing comes easy, and sacrifice and commitment is always a requirement to make your goals achievable. The only difference is your hunger, desire, and your sheer will to stay on course even when life gets tough. You know you are on track when obstacles come your way and your commitment never wavers from your ultimate goal. As a result, your character strengthens and you become better, stronger, smarter, and wiser in your pursuit for a great life.

Power of Affirmation

*"I choose to stay committed and I choose to stay on course because every step I take gets me closer to an awesome life.
I CAN, I WILL, I MUST!"*

DAY 12
DREAM – WITH INTENTION AND EXECUTION

Have you heard of the word expression, "Dreaming is for free"? Most people doubt themselves and never realize that dreams can be reality. Everyone has a dream, the only difference is whether you become relentless and chase it or remain wallowing in self-pity. The majority of successful people have a dream with intention and execution. What made them so significant is that they wrote it down, visualized it, planned, and executed. Start dreaming with intention. Don't just think about it, do the necessary things to make it happen. Dream is your fuel and the key is your action.

Power of Affirmation

*"I have a dream. My thoughts and action will make it a reality.
I CAN, I WILL, I MUST!"*

DAY 13
FOCUS – EQUALS RESULTS

What you focus on and what your thoughts are determine what you will become and where your destination will be. This means, if you constantly focus on the wrong things, on negativity, problems, the loss opportunities, these will be the outcome of your life. A negative life or mind can never bring you a great and positive life. So how would we change this type of process? Start by focusing on the good things, see yourself succeeding, build your thoughts and mindset that opportunities are constantly coming to you, and focus on your life being wonderful. The outcome of this process is you become more solution-focused, more resourceful than ever, and your attitude becomes more lighter. You can succeed in anything in life!

Power of Affirmation

*"I am focus I am determined.
I CAN, I WILL, I MUST!"*

DAY 14
DETERMINATION – BRINGS YOUR DRIVE

Determination is that will power that moves you to your goals, dreams, and life's passion. It also gives so much impact to do great things that you thought you couldn't do! Determination leads to more certainty, the ability to breakthrough doubts, freedom from fears and failures, and ultimately to your personal success. Every great leader, athlete, entrepreneur, and person who serves their country shares this common passion. They will charge forward with determination in their mind, heart, and their decision to act. It's their willingness of attitude that allows them to complete difficult tasks.

What are your fears or things that are holding you back that could prevent you from succeeding? What is the area that you need to stop doing, and start doing in your life? When you realize and are aware of what it is, this gives you the power to own it and work it with confidence and with the right attitude, strategy, plan and determination you can thrive.

Power of Affirmation

*"I have determination in my eyes and will power to make things happen in my life.
I CAN, I WILL, I MUST!"*

DAY 15
PURPOSE – TO THRIVE

Many people nowadays are not certain, unsure, and lack confident about their purpose? Most people believe in the standard process of acquiring an education, and then finding a job, raise a family and retire. In simple terms you eat, sleep, work and repeat this mundane cycle, then suddenly you realize you have lost 5 years of your life. Time will always pass and you are powerless to change your past, but you can change your future by making a choice to stand up for yourself to live a purposeful life. The question is how? Firstly having awareness and taking responsibility. All it takes is your decision and your firm self-belief to thrive in life knowing you are heading to the right direction.

Power of Affirmation

My purpose is to fulfil my life with gratitude, hope and everything that is in stored for me I CAN, I WILL, I MUST!

DAY 16
EMPOWER – OTHERS IS ONE OF THE GREATEST ASSETS

There is a leader in all of us and our perspective about leadership all differs depending on our past experiences. Leadership is neither by title nor by the position given, it's taking the lead to live life at its fullest. It is harnessing the power from within, having the full confidence in your God-given ability that you can achieve and win in life. The ultimate most fulfilling part in contribution is empowering others by placing a mark in this world to influence and make a difference to those who are in need. This act of valor displays character, strength, humility and these quality traits of a leader is all within us, it does not matter how big or small it is by empowering others, that we ourselves become empowered.

Power of Affirmation

*"I will empower others and contribute so they can experience abundance.
I CAN, I WILL, I MUST!"*

DAY 17
GOALS – TO GIVE YOU THE CUTTING EDGE

When you hear and think about goals, there are five types of people. Person 1 only makes goals when it is close to the end or beginning of the year, which is called New Year's resolution. Person 2 only makes goals when the person has to at work. Person 3 only thinks about making goals someday for themselves. Person 4 does not believe in goals because they know themselves they can't achieve it. Finally, Person 5 decides to make simple, measurable, achievable, realistic, timely goals in their career, family, health, finance, and personal life. After reviewing the 5 types of people, which category do you fit in? A goal without a plan is just a thought. If you want a head start with your goals, start placing short, mid, and long-term goals with a specific date you want to achieve. This is another tool to get you closer to your dreams and success you want in your life.

Power of Affirmation

"I will not settle for less. I will settle for abundance. I choose not to procrastinate and start placing realistic and achievable goals that I will not give up and stand up fighting for. I CAN, I WILL, I MUST!"

DAY 18
SUCCESS – GOES MULTIPLE WAYS

If we were to narrow down the one determinant to success, it solely lies on taking massive ACTION!

Nothing is ever done without it. The word alone carries so much weight, because if you study every successful person in this world, they remain action-oriented despite the hardships and failures that may come their way. Success is within us if we see ourselves successful, having a positive mindset, taking the initiative to place a plan and action. Whichever is your definition of success, make it happen, it's only you that has the power to choose and act.

Power of Affirmation

"My goals, dreams, aspiration and the abundance of life is greater than my current circumstances.
I CAN, I WILL, I MUST!"

DAY 19
CONSISTENCY – IS THE KEY TO INNOVATION & CREATIVITY

Where there is commitment and competency, consistency runs wild. This means the more you commit and stay competent in what you are pursuing without wavering and fearlessly eliminating all negative noises, consistency will provide clarity and certainty. The benefits of consistency will enhance your work to be smarter and will cause you to have a razor sharp focus. So the question that will come to your mind is how to stay consistent. The answer is have a bigger reason of why, to motivate and capture your passion. If you want to excel in your career, relationship, health, wealth and personal life, you must bring in the elements of excellence, absolute focus, hard-core determination and uncompromising attitude. By consistently moving forward, you will reap the rewards. Because what you will sow and invest, you will reap the harvest.

Power of Affirmation

"I have total confidence in my abilities and consistency to follow-through in my life. I CAN, I WILL, I MUST!"

DAY 20
PERSONAL GROWTH – FOR IMPACTING CHANGES

We live in a fast-paced world, technology rising to where imaginations becomes reality. Think back 10-20 years ago when smartphones, tablets, PCs, apps, smart watches, wireless earphones, mp3 players, and personal devices didn't exist. Fast-forward to the present and these devices are now in the palm of our hands and everyone is in the craze for the new exciting latest new upgrades. If we put it in perspective that technology will continue to grow and find faster ways to better society, we should look into our lives the same way, finding ways how we can innovate and be the better version. We should look for ways to improve and have purposeful lives otherwise will we stay behind to our old mindsets and habits. Take initiative to follow-through to changing your lives in your mindsets, identifying areas in what you need to improve. Personal growth will lead to impacting changes and it comes to our thought processes to decide to act.

Power of Affirmation

*"I will commit to constantly learn and grow as a person.
I CAN, I WILL, I MUST!"*

DAY 21
YES

You are human, if you make mistakes or fail in some areas, the great news it is not forever nor is it permanent to be a failure. Your choices and decision to act can change your life significantly. It is saying yes to yourself, and believing you do deserve the best things in life, your career, health, wealth, love and in happiness. Sometimes we feel that things are not going the way it should go or the way you envisioned, don't worry you are on the right track. How you ask? Firstly, you chose not to give up. Secondly, you are fighting relentlessly till you win. Finally, you know that your dreams and the life you want is bigger than obstacles in your way. By reading, absorbing, affirming, believing, achieving and completing day 21 this shows you are committed to make changes for an awesome life, to be stronger than ever, to have more clarity and certainty with enormous confidence for personal success. You have it in you.

Power of Affirmation

*"I say yes to myself,
I CAN, I WILL, I MUST!'*

CONGRATULATIONS!

Well done on completing 21 Days of Thrive Challenge. The next step is share your thoughts, and encourage your friends and family about the 21 Days of Thrive. Use social media (Facebook, Instagram, and Twitter) and use the hashtag #21daysofthrive and don't forget to tag @gezperezthrive, so your family and friends will also be inspired to cultivate a great life.

ABOUT GEZ PEREZ

Gez is passionate about empowering people to take charge of their lives and take it to the next level so they can achieve personal success. His focus is to serve and inspire people so they can achieve and unlock their true potential for greatness.

Gez provides insightful proven strategies in challenging people to thrive in any area of their lives and makes an impact by developing their passion, influence and confidence. This has resulted in clients witnessing how they are able to become the best version of themselves and achieve breakthrough results.

Gez is a HBDI Practitioner, Master Coach through Life & Leadership, Certified Professional (DISC, Motivators & Emotional Quotient) and Motivational Speaker. He has spoken internationally in South East Asia & North America.

For the past many years, he has worked with market-leading corporate companies in around Australia. He has a strong background in communications, Client Services, Project Management and Information Technology.

Gez has been featured in various media platforms. Owner of GP Thrive International and Co-Founder of Arise Business Network.

PROGRAMS BY GEZ PEREZ

Motivation without the Hype

One Day Workshop Event

You can experience and learn by discovering key insights in focusing on empowering strategies in a "live" setting. This is ideal for conferences, conventions, corporate retreats, and in-house meetings and events.

The MWTH one-day program includes:

- Sessions on how to set and achieve your personal, business, financial, and health goals with in-depth action plans and templates.

- Learn the mindset and tools to equip you for success. Be able to master your habits, time and focus that brings out the best in you.

- Proven methods and systems for you to enjoy life with the balance of work and family.

For details and scheduling contact teamthrive@gezperez.com

THRIVE FORWARD COACHING PROGRAM

"Achieve, exceed, and succeed in your results with inspiring coaching."

This is a proven system to help you thrive in focusing on your influence, impact, and strengths, so you can unleash your greatness through life and business for success.

    This program offers personal group coaching for professionals and business people who are ready to take their lives to the next level. You will learn how to set and achieve your goals in every aspect of your life and gain key insights of step by step process to double your results.

    Each group will meet on assigned dates for coaching under an experienced Thrive Coach. Its purpose is to unlock personal high performance, execute with action, collaborate through networking, review personal progress, and continuously self-improve. This in turn will enhance personal success and triple the outcomes. In addition you'll learn how to be more productive, eliminate procrastination, and take decisive action.

    To find out more information contact teamthrive@gezperez.com

www.ingramcontent.com/pod-product-compliance
Lightning Source LLC
Chambersburg PA
CBHW071438080526
44587CB00014B/1906